D0948610

AFRICAN NATIONALISM

THE AUTHOR

Ndabaningi Sithole

AFRICAN NATIONALISM

SECOND EDITION

1969
OXFORD UNIVERSITY PRESS
LONDON NAIROBI IBADAN
New York

LIBRARY — LUTHERAN SCHOOL
OF THEOLOGY AT CHICAGO

DT
31
.S55
1968

African Nationalism was first published by
Oxford University Press, Cape Town, in 1959.
Second edition published in London 1968.

© Oxford University Press 1959, 1968

Printed in the United States of America

CONTENTS

AFRICAN NATIONALISM

INTRODUCTION

During my stay in the United States of America I was confronted by what some of my American friends said about African nationalism, which at that time was just beginning to be felt throughout the length and breadth of the continent of Africa, and which was also just beginning to make fairly sensational international headlines. The big question which everyone was asking was: Is Africa ready for sovereign independence? The majority greatly doubted that Africa was ready. Some regarded the rise of African nationalism as a bad omen for the white man in Africa. Some felt that since the white man had opened up Africa there was no reason for the African, at least at that time, to be talking of ruling himself. They felt that the African should have been silent over the question of self-rule since the white man had done, so they argued, an excellent piece of work—he had opened up Africa. I was greatly agitated by such attitudes, and I felt I should explain what African nationalism really was; and so it was that in 1957 I wrote my *African Nationalism* which was first published in June 1959 and was later translated into six other languages.

At the time I wrote *African Nationalism*, which was an attempt to justify the upsurging force which was swaying the entire continent, there were only eight independent African countries. Ethiopia, which has been independent since 1040 B.C., except for a short period—1936–1941—when the Italians occupied it, and Liberia, which has been independent since 1847, are the two oldest independent African countries. Egypt (now the United Arab Republic) became independent in 1922, while Libya became independent in 1951, and Tunisia, Sudan, and Morocco in 1956. Ghana became independent in 1957. It was during this year that I began and finished my book, which was, as I have said, a justification for African nationalism. It took me over four months to write it.

But since that date—1957—events in Africa have moved very rapidly, far beyond what I had anticipated. The map of Africa has changed considerably. Instead of only eight independent African countries, 1966 found 38 independent African countries! It is no longer necessary to try to justify African nationalism. That has already been done. It has justified itself by its own achievements. It is no longer a force of the future as it was in 1957, when I first wrote *African Nationalism*. It is now a force of the immediate past. Its main headwaters which swept away colonialism and imperialism were discharged in the year 1960 when seventeen African countries became fully independent. General de Gaulle—that shrewd, sagacious politician and statesman whose thinking was grounded in realism—greatly helped in the fortunes of African nationalism when in the years 1958–1960 he offered the French colonies independence if they so decided. Since the independence peak of 1960 thirteen more African countries have become independent, and the struggle for liberating Southern Africa has started. Present events on the continent of Africa seem to point only to one thing, and that is, Africa is destined to rule herself. Whatever enclaves of foreign rule are still found in Africa, it is now a question of time before these foreign enclaves are wiped out from the face of the map of Africa, just as we predicted in 1957 that 'the domination space' was rapidly shrinking everywhere in Africa. Only 'the friendship race' is rapidly expanding. Those who still hope to dominate Africa might as well rethink their position in their own interests since the merciless wheel of history is now turning with greater velocity in the direction of a free and independent Africa. It cannot be reversed in the direction of a European-ruled Africa. History has ordained it that way. The sooner those who still dominate some parts of Africa realize this the better for them. Events are following an irreversible course.

As a result of these irreversible events which took an accelerated pace from 1956 onward, only 30,000,000 African people are still not independent out of the present population of 260,000,000. This is to say, 88 per cent. of the African population is now free from foreign rule. The free countries of Africa have now a much smaller task of liberating the remaining 12 per cent. of the African population from the clutches of foreign rule. The free forces of Africa should now find the task of liberating Africa much easier than at any time in the history of the liberation of Africa.

In terms of the soil of Africa the present facts can only mean this: that most of the land of Africa, which is the real wealth of any nation and any people, now belongs to the African nations and the African people themselves. The 11,500,000 square miles of Africa which had been stolen by foreigners have been now restored to their rightful owners. Only about 2,000,000 square miles of Africa's land are still under absolute control of foreigners. This is to say about one-sixth of African land is still under foreign control, and it is a question of time before this 'unfree' land comes under African control. That which the land of Africa yields will now be used first and foremost for the benefit of the African peoples who will no longer be looking for crumbs dropping from the tables of foreign rulers. The enormous mineral wealth which is locked up in the very bowels of Africa will now be extracted first for the benefit of the African people. Foreign interests will no longer come first but second. This is as it should be. American interests must come first in America. European interests must come first in Europe. Russian interests must come first in Russia. Chinese interests must come first in the People's Republic of China. And this has been the genius of African nationalism that African interests now come first in Africa. The injustices of many decades have been righted not only to the good of the peoples of Africa but also the peoples of the world, since the existence of an 'exploitation continent' is in itself a basic cause of war among those who feel they are entitled for one reason or another to exercise fully their self-given 'exploitation rights'.

That 230,000,000 Africans are now free has a significance which it would take a separate volume to explain. At the turn of the present century the African population that will have been born between now and then will be living in freedom and independence. They will walk with their heads held up in full human dignity since Africa for the most part has now ceased to breed 'unfree' men and women. She now breeds free men and women who no longer have to bow to foreign rulers. People now live for themselves and not for foreign rulers. They now get educated for their own sakes. They can now develop at their own pace without having to be controlled by the temperament of foreign rulers. They are now people. They feel they are people. Men and women of other nationalities and races now regard them as full persons. They now belong to their country. They can now say 'Our Country'. No amount of money or wealth could have given them this feeling. Only freedom and independence gives this priceless feeling.

When my publishers asked me at the beginning of 1966 to revise *African Nationalism*, I found it difficult to alter a word here, a sentence there. So much had happened. For instance, when I first wrote the book, the chapter headed 'The Cracking Myth' made a great deal of sense, since, indeed, the myth was then cracking but still holding together. It had not fallen asunder. But today it is no longer a question of 'The Cracking Myth' but rather 'The Cracked Myth'. When I first wrote the book my main task was, as I have said earlier, to explain the rising African nationalism, but as I revise it today that is no longer my task. My task has been to explain how African nationalism has achieved its objectives as evidenced by the emergence of thirty more fully independent African countries. To do this I have had to increase the chapters from the original thirteen to twenty-one chapters.

As I stand, as it were, on the shoulders of my 1957 *African Nationalism* I can see farther afield than I did then, and as I have since then actively participated in the liberation struggle, I have had to give my revised book a special treatment. There are four sections altogether. The first is Part 1—'Autobiographical Matters'; then come Part 2—'Factors of Nationalism'; Part 3— 'The Philosophy of White Supremacy'; and Part 4—'Nationalism's Problems'.

Part 1 is mostly autobiographical. This is, I felt, a necessary background to my main subject—nationalism. The autobiographical account typifies in many ways the pattern African nationalists have followed all over Africa. Part 2 is an exposition of the factors that contributed to the rise of African nationalism. Part 3 deals with the nature of white supremacy, which stood over and against the African people who sired African nationalism, which in turn was responsible for the liquidation of white supremacy. Part 4 deals with the problems which have been raised by the fact of Africa's sovereign independence.

Events in Africa defy any pattern. Things seem to sort themselves out. Africa moves not according to the pulse of any other continent. She moves according to her own pulse. She is the only one who can know where the shoe pinches. Those who had thought it would take many centuries before Africa became independent have been proved wrong. They made the fatal mistake of judging her by their own standards which were external and irrelevant to her. What determined and still determines the course of events in Africa is the African's own definition of his own situation, not the foreigner's definition of Africa's situation. This has been the fundamental fact underlying the course of events in Africa.

There are soon to be only ten African countries which will not be independent. These are Angola, Cabinda, French Somaliland, Mozambique, Portuguese Guinea, Rhodesia, South Africa, South-West Africa, Spanish Guinea, and Spanish Sahara. African liberatory forces are busily engaged in an effort to dislodge foreign rule in all these remaining non-independent African countries, and the international forces of freedom and majority rule are on their side. It augurs very well for African independence, but very badly for the remaining foreign rulers.

One of the greatest blessings in the situation of independent Africa is the absence of racial animosity. In independent Africa nowhere have white people been subjected to persecution as a racial group. Africans are not interested in anything else except to run their own countries and to control their own destinies. White populations are on the increase in many independent African countries, and the colour bar which the white man had introduced in Africa has been dealt a deathblow in all the thirty-eight independent African countries; it lives only in South Africa, Rhodesia, Mozambique, Angola, and South-West Africa, where the white man still holds sway. The day is fast coming when the entire continent of Africa will be freed from any colour bar, and the champions of the colour bar will realize that

> All people of the earth
> Share but one common birth . . . .

No human fellowship, no human sympathy, no human understanding, no human co-operation, no human respect, no human sanctity, and no human virtue can exist under conditions of the colour bar or white supremacy. The white man in Africa failed to teach this big lesson of human fellowship—the oneness of mankind—and if free and independent Africa cannot teach it the European-ruled African countries cannot and must not be expected to teach it. Foreign rulers are only interested in the exploitation of the natural and human resources of Africa. They are not interested in the fundamental things that touch the very core of human existence. Only the free citizens of Africa will worry about the fundamental things of life. And may history never have the occasion to record that free and independent Africa ever descended so low as to practise the colour bar—the practice of punishing a man because of the colour of his skin. Nothing could be more sinful against the entire human race and against God Himself.

I have revised my *African Nationalism* during an indefinite detention. After the white settlers of Rhodesia seized independence on 11 November 1965, they locked up all African nationalists in detention. Advocate Edson Sithole, who has spent over five years in restriction and detention, and who is at present my fellow-detainee, has been kind enough to read through this revision. I feel greatly indebted to his critical reading and useful comments but he is fully exonerated from any shortcomings of this work. I take the full responsibility for any flaws that may appear in this work.

PART ONE

Autobiographical Matters

CHAPTER 1

Finding My Way

My father, Jim Sithole, at the age of eighteen, left Gazaland, his home district, to seek adventure and fortune in Umtali. He was only four months in Umtali when he decided to leave for Salisbury, where he worked as a 'kitchen boy' for two years. It was in Salisbury that he acquired a smattering of English and Afrikaans, which he could neither write nor read, just as he was unable to read or write any of the existing vernaculars of Southern Rhodesia. Allured by fortune stories told to him by his home boys who worked in Gwelo, he left Salisbury and found work with the Grand Hotel, Gwelo. Still spurred on by his love of adventure and fortune, he resigned his post and went to work in Bulawayo.

One fine morning as he was running an errand, an intelligent-looking country girl drew his attention. He halted, as he always says, 'to admire the killing beauty of this girl'. But the urgency of the errand demanded that he go on without stopping. He stood torn between his master's orders and his heart's desire. He soon forgot all about the errand and one and a half hours passed by unnoticed. He took the particulars of this girl—her name Siyapi Tshuma, her home district Nyamandlovu. The girl was pleased that she had favourably impressed someone as handsome as my father.

Five visits to Nyamandlovu during week-ends soon rewarded my father's efforts. Six months after the engagement my father was married to Siyapi Tshuma according to native rites. On 31 July 1920 I was born to my father and mother. I had a low mud-and-pole hut with a dirt floor for a maternity clinic, bits of old skins for my blanket, and a folded buck-skin for my pillow. On the same day that I arrived I was made to inhale the smoke from a burning goat's horn so that no evil would befall me. This smoking process was continued for three weeks and after that I was considered immune from all the evil intentions of our neighbours.

I grew up to the age of seven playing hide-and-seek and making clay oxen. At night we gathered round Granny to hear her tell us the wonderful stories of old. Granny was a thrilling story-teller, and it was not easy to forget her stories—so vivid, so appealing, so hair-raising, and told with such animation. She could tell a story, then introduce some singing, then continue the story, and even dance the story if it had some dancing in it. We could join the singing and the dancing. 'Behave yourself, or no story from Granny' became a real warning that made us behave ourselves.

From the age of seven onwards my life was spent among bellowing bulls, lowing oxen, bleating sheep and goats, and baaing lambs. Herding was one of those irksome drudgeries. Like all other boys I disliked it. I envied men because they had done their stint. I longed to grow into a man quickly and be done with it.

There were many difficulties incidental to herding. Hunger was the commonest hardship. We had breakfast at about ten in the morning. Then we drove the cattle to the pasture, usually between five and ten miles away from home. Except for the wild fruit when in season, we did not have anything to eat until late in the evening. We made many silent prayers that the sun should set quickly so that we might return home to fill our empty bellies. We were not allowed to bring the cattle home before sunset. The next trouble came from the senior boys. They were the bosses and we, the juniors, did all the hard work of herding. They gave orders and we carried them out. We were forbidden on pain of severe thrashing to disclose to people at home any unsavoury happenings in the forest, which usually included senior boys' bullying, cruelty, and garden-raiding.

I remember one day when Zenzo, our senior boy, warned us, 'Don't tell anybody at home that we have taken water melons from Menzelwa's garden.' We all promised not to. As we sat round the fire with some of our elders I proudly remarked to Zenzo, 'You thought we were going to tell the old people that we took some water melons. You see, I haven't.' Poor me! I learned the lesson the hard way. The next day every boy gave me some whipping on the legs saying, 'We don't say such things at home.' I pleaded, 'I will never do it again.'

One day as we were herding cattle, we saw a very strange thing. We thought it was a hut, but then it was moving very fast. In great fear we dashed into the forest near by, but curiosity checked our fear. We halted, and with panting hearts we carefully hid ourselves behind the bushes and made our observations from there. The strange moving hut then pulled up. 'It has seen us!' we cried in a chorus and rushed into the depths of the forest. We ran home as fast as our legs could carry us. Fearfully we reported the incident, and those who had been to Bulawayo and who had seen motor-cars nearly split their sides with laughter!

Like most of the children of our district, I had *amabetshu*—two skin aprons, one covering the back and the other the front. These *amabetshu* were tied round the waist so that they looked more like two rough triangular patches than clothing. The whole trunk remained bare. On cold days an old sack served as my overcoat, and on rainy days the same sack was used as a raincoat, by the simple method of pushing in one corner against the opposite corner so that the two corners stuck out at one point forming a kind of hood for my head. Round my neck was an *intebe*—a talisman, supposed to protect me from the evil spirits believed to dwell in the big dark forests of Nyamandlovu. Round my waist was yet another *intebe* supposed to protect me from the evil intentions of our neighbours. These articles constituted the entire stock of my clothing.

One chilly morning I accompanied my uncle to the dip-tank. The whole purpose of my going to the dip-tank was to see the white man who was said to be branding the cattle there. I had never seen a white face before. I was curious to see one. He was a tall, hefty, fearful figure. I grasped my uncle's arm firmly at the sight of this most extraordinary human being. His eyes moved quickly like those of a leopard we had seen one day. Everyone was paying attention to him. He was the master of the situation. Then he took a red-hot iron and pressed it on the cow's hind quarters, and the cow made an eerie roar. I was terribly frightened. I never learned to like this branding white man who burnt good cows for sport.

At the end of 1930 my father left Nyamandlovu for Shabani. We walked all the way from Nyamandlovu to Bembesi Railway Station—a distance of about fifty miles. I was excited at the idea of seeing the train. I had never seen it before. It took us two days to get to Bembesi. There I awaited the arrival of the train with bated breath.

Father bought us clothes for the first time. We threw away our *amabetshu*. I struggled into my khaki shorts shaking with great excitement, and I endeavoured to put on my khaki shirt. At last the struggle was over. There I stood in my new clothes smiling excitedly and unable to believe that that was myself. I put my hands deep in my pockets like some important little man. My wife Canaan and I have never passed Bembesi without her insisting on my getting down and looking for my *amabetshu*.

'Puff! puff! puff! puff!' came the sound from the distance. I became dead still with attention. Here now was the real thing the idea of which had greatly excited me, raised my hopes, whetted my sense of pleasure, eased my otherwise long and tedious journey, made me feel I was going to a better world, and made me forget all about Granny and her stories. I listened fearfully to the terrifying noise; curiosity changed to fear, excitement to anxiety. I was bewildered and puzzled by this strange and terrific noise. I looked in the distance and out came the huge black monster 'vomiting' and 'coughing' great clouds of black smoke. It seemed to make straight for me. 'God! Save me from the monster!' I cried, dashing away from it. I was making for Granny's home where no such threatening monsters dwelt. I longed for the peace and security in my Granny's mud hut. I must have covered more than a quarter of a mile before my father finally caught and carried me kicking and struggling. I would have jumped out of the train had he not prevented me. Fearfully I sat in the train and tightly held to my mother's arm. I became the centre of laughter, pity, and inquiry. I provided good sport for the passengers.

We reached Shabani in due course. The sight of row upon row of neatly thatched huts greatly impressed me. I had never seen anything like it before. Added to my bewilderment were the numerous tribes in this compound. They spoke different languages and observed different customs. Among these were the Makaranga, the Vazezuru, the Vamanyika, the Mashangana, the Manyasa, the Machawa, the Masena, the Marubare, and a few other tribes. Fortune-hunting had brought them all together.

Life was comparatively easy here. There was no herding. We spent most of our time playing in and around the compound, visiting local stores, exploring workshops, sliding down the big asbestos dumps, digging holes in the old and solid dumps, and on Saturdays and Sundays we acted as caddies for European golfers. It was such great fun that I soon forgot all about Nyamandlovu and Granny's thrilling stories told by the fireside.

In this compound there was a school run by the British Methodist Church (then called Wesleyan Church). In 1932 I started going to school. I went to school because I had nothing else to do, and because I thought it was a good thing to do what other children were doing. Our lessons were the usual three Rs, Bible, hygiene, vegetable-gardening, clay-modelling, and simple woodwork.

We had a very strict teacher who did not spare his whip if he thought we needed it. He used the whip to get us to master the lesson quickly and thoroughly, to make us quiet when we were noisy, to get good attendance, and to make us come to school at the right time.

There was magic in our teacher's whip. It achieved exactly what he wanted.

My father was not interested in my schooling, but my mother was. She had gone to school for only two weeks before she revolted against her teacher's constant whipping and quit the school. That was the only time she went to school.

Despite our teacher's constant whippings we liked our school. Learning and whipping became inseparable. We all accepted the fact that without whipping there could be no real learning.

At the end of 1932, following the persistent advice of my father, I left school and went to work for a Mr. Bell. I was employed as a 'kitchen boy'. I used to look after their five-year-old boy. Mrs. Bell taught me how to wash myself regularly, how to clean my clothes and my teeth, keep my finger-nails short and clean, and how to keep her Charlie clean. For the slightest dirt she saw she flared up. Sometimes I honestly believed she was mad. 'If the dirt is mine, what business has she to worry about it?' I often wondered.

In 1935 I received a letter from a cousin of mine, London Sithole, who was five years my junior. The letter had been written in English. Although I had continued my schooling by attending night school, I had not progressed beyond the Sub B grade. I could not read the letter; my pride was deeply injured. 'I can't read what the young boy writes!' I cried in sheer disgust. The thought of being surpassed by someone five years younger than I was was unbearable. It stung my soul, and for weeks, as we say in Ndebele, 'it ate me from inside'. I decided to go to London's boarding-school. At the end of July, after many pleas from my employer that I should not go away, I was finally released.

'I want to go to school,' I told my father.

'You lazy fellow. Go back and work,' he growled. Then he reminded me of the many kindnesses that Mrs. Hatfield (for whom I was by then working) had shown me, and told me that he would have preferred me to die in her service. 'Tomorrow,' he said, biting his teeth with indignation, 'you go back to Mrs. Hatfield and work. I don't want to hear anything about your school.'

I knew my father had spoken and that he would not take back what he had said. 'Yes, father,' I agreed with him.

'That's a boy,' he said, softening down.

The next morning I got all my clothes and blankets ready. Instead of going to Mrs. Hatfield's house I found myself going to Dadaya Mission by train.

'Did you apply?' asked the missionary-in-charge at Dadaya Mission. This was the Rev. Garfield Todd, later the Prime Minister of Southern Rhodesia.

'No, Nkosi,' I said.

'This is August, my son,' he said sadly, 'and we take pupils at the beginning of the year.'

I was dumb, puzzled, disappointed, and I felt tears in my eyes. In sheer pity for me, however, the missionary accepted me. The head-mistress, Mrs. Grace Todd, placed me in Standard One. I had saved money but not more than £2. Fees were only 10s. a year! I paid in my fees and I became a boarder. Now perhaps my wounded pride would heal up!

I was behind in many things. My arithmetic was atrocious, my written English was bad, although my oral English was good and my English reading not so bad. I had been used to answer those in authority by 'Yes, Nkosi' or 'Yes, Missus', but now I had to learn the new way of saying 'Yes, Mfundisi' (that is, 'Reverend') or 'Yes, Nkosikazi' ('Madam-of-honour'). I used to mix up the old and the new way, to the great amusement of both staff and students.

Life here was very interesting in many ways. There were the Christian Endeavour Society, the Debating Society, the camp-fires, and the Sunday services. We liked classroom work better than out-side work. We erroneously held the view that education meant exemption from all forms of manual work; to us education meant reading books, writing and talking English, and doing arithmetic. We thought that the ability to do these things was the mark of the only true education. To use one's hands to earn one's living, we thought, was below one's dignity. We resented all forms of manual work.

Perhaps an explanation of our attitude to manual work is not out of place here. At our homes we had done a lot of ploughing, planting, weeding, and harvesting; we had hewn wood and drawn water; we had tended sheep, goats, and cattle; we had done a hundred and one odd jobs. We knew how to do these things. We had come to school, not for these, but for those things we did not know. What we knew was not education; education was what we did not know. If we had had our way we would have unanimously voted for 'Only classroom work, and no manual work'. We wanted, as we said in Ndebele, 'to learn the book until it remained in our hands, to speak English until we could speak it through our nose'.

The missionary here was ideally suited for handling boys of our dispositions. By his own example and precept he taught us the dignity of manual labour. He used his own hands in the fields, in his own back-yard, and he washed his own car. He moulded bricks with us, hoed the fields with us, and did many odd jobs with us. Gradually our attitude toward manual work changed for the better.

The same year that I was admitted to Dadaya Mission, I professed repentance and acceptance of Christ. I did not accept Christ as a personal Redeemer, or because of a deep conviction of Christ's way, but because I thought that since other boys and girls had accepted Him, it would be a nice thing for me to do the same thing. Not to be baptized was a kind of social stigma that goaded many boys and girls into professed repentance. Christ to me meant no more and no less than a social badge.

In 1936 my little savings were exhausted and I was compelled to remain on the Mission Station, working holiday after holiday. It was not an easy thing to remain on the Mission Station every holiday. It was a great stigma as it revealed the poor financial circumstances of my parents. Youthful pride that refuses to accept disagreeable facts about one's poor parents, and chooses to paint one's poor parents in brighter colours than they really are, made me feel sharply what it meant to be born of poor parents. Like all others who were in the same boat with me, I was held in great contempt but I soon got used to the game. I knew only too well that going home meant no school fees and that this meant no schooling, but I liked schooling.

During this time several girls came to Dadaya Mission to seek refuge. These girls had been pledged, or forced into marriage, by their own parents. Refusing to marry where they did not love, they deserted their parents and took refuge on the Mission Station. The missionary-in-charge befriended them and cared for them.

'But are you going to receive *lobola* for these girls?' I asked him one day.

'No, but why?' he asked me.

'Well, I see you care for them as well as if you are going to get something from them,' I said.

'No, I won't get a farthing, Ndabaningi.'

'But why all this bother then?'

'I am doing this for Christ's sake.'

'Christ's sake!' I cried. 'What's that?'

'Well, Christ wants everyone to be free, to marry whom they choose, not to be forced. I'm doing this because I want to do Christ's will. That is why I am a Christian.'

This was news to me. I, too, decided to help others without expecting anything in return. Here again I was just aping the great missionary, but I was growing in my Christian experience.

In 1937 the missionary-in-charge asked me to help him in the dispensary. I gladly helped him for the next three years. I noticed that the missionary lived for all those in need of help. If there was any case of illness and it came to his notice he would attend to it immediately. Sometimes when I was overworked I felt like telling him so, but I was ashamed to tell him so because he was more overworked than I was.

Fire-burns were the worst cases that we had to deal with. One day a woman brought her baby, over whom a boiling pot had tipped. That little baby, hardly two months old, was a frightful and repulsive spectacle. She died in my hands while I was trying to help her. Another charming little girl, a little over four years of age, had all her abdomen burnt. Her drunken mother had been cooking *sadza* while she lay by the fire. The pot tipped over and the porridge spilled on the girl. She died within eight hours of admission. All these things kept the missionary busy. 'For Christ's sake', he kept on saying as he went about helping these people. Gradually I began to see, and my faith grew from mere imitation to something real.

From my limited Christian experience, I have come to realize that Christ's way of life is something that grows from within. It is not something that grows on the individual. First we see our need for a Saviour, and after letting him in we begin to grow like Him as we see Him in the Bible or lived by other lives. I began to realize that to accept Christ was to allow the gradual unfolding of a nobler purpose as manifested in Christ's life. The Sunday School also helped me in getting a real Christian experience and fellowship.

In 1939, when I was nineteen, I finished my Standard Six at Dadaya Mission. I was highest in my class. I was awarded a Beit Bursary of £10 tenable at Waddilove Training Institution for two years. I would have left school if this award had not been made, unless someone else had come to my aid.

In many ways Waddilove was a stimulating place. There were several departments—building, carpentry, theology, teacher training, and the Central Primary School. The Rev. George Hay Pluke was the principal of the school and under him fell the departmental heads. Our professional teacher in the Teacher Training Department was Mr. William Tregidgo. We all admired him. He was strict and thorough, fair and firm, and demanded the same from us. By his own example he taught us to be punctual. It is twenty-five years since we were taught by him, and through the corridors of time and space I can still hear him saying slowly in his clear bell-like voice, 'Hammer it, hammer it, and hammer it, into the children's minds.'

The principal taught us the principles of education. Mr. Pluke was opposed to any form of corporal punishment, and he taught us not to use it. We did not agree with him. At home old people had not spared the rod to spoil the children; at my previous Central Primary School whipping had been used as part of disciplining the students. Apparently, I had come out the better for it. I warmly supported corporal punishment, and as most of us were not adherents of the 'no-whip' theory, we secretly thrashed the children we taught during our practical teaching periods.

Mr. Pluke was very interested in cultural reading. 'The trouble with you, Ndabaningi, is that you always read for examinations and not for pleasure. Learn to read for pleasure.' Sometimes I nearly told him, 'Pleasure won't make me pass.' But I soon caught on to what he meant. He laid good foundations for my cultural reading. Under his directions and encouragement I read over fifty books during my two years at Waddilove—English classics mostly: *David Copperfield, Oliver Twist, Silas Marner, The Vicar of Wakefield, The Last Days of Pompeii, Prester John,* and others in their simplified and abridged forms.

At Waddilove Sunday School we were led by Miss Marjorie Baker, who was very devoted to spiritual matters. I was one of her Sunday School teachers. She taught us during preparation classes to pray hard over lessons before we taught them. She taught us the value of strictly private prayers.

When I finished my teaching course at Waddilove I was sent to a kraal school where I taught lower classes. My head was buzzing with private studies. I wanted more education. If I had had money I would have gone to a secondary school. Amid most forbidding surroundings I did my private studies side by side with my teaching and was glad that a year of real hard work rewarded me with National Junior Certificate. In those days, particularly the first half of the 1940s, the possession of such academic qualifications was a rare achievement. After my success more teachers enrolled for National Junior Certificate. They were no longer content to be spectators.

One day as I went about my teaching, I lost my temper with one of my Standard Two girls who always came late to school and always smiled whenever I told her not to smile; she did not seem to care about the matter. I had punished her but there was no apparent reform. I was reluctant to proceed to corporal punishment, not because I had believed what Mr. Pluke had tried to teach us, but because I was young and I feared the reactions of the girl's father, who had the evil repute of a witch-doctor. But in my anger—that temporary madness—I soundly thrashed the girl.

'Teacher, you will die!' cried many children in pity for me. 'You'll die! You'll die!' They were all death-scared. What a strong hold witchcraft has on the minds of the people! Children grow up in it and it is almost impossible to dissuade them against witchcraft when they grow old.

Late in the afternoon the girl's father came. He was a tall muscular man, not less than six feet. He looked contemptuously at me. I felt heavily his presence.

'Why did you beat my daughter?' he asked.

I tried to explain as best I could, but he would not listen.

'You won't see the next harvest,' he threatened.

By this statement he meant that he was going to invoke his evil spirits which would see to it that I was put out of existence mysteriously. I knew what he meant. I had heard numerous stories of his nocturnal duties. He had bewitched men, women, and children in the neighbourhood. Educated and uneducated, Christian and heathen, young and old, rich and poor, all believed implicitly that this man had supernatural power over human life. I had never been threatened in this way before. I felt uneasy although I had never believed in mysterious killing by witch-doctors.

Providence has equipped each one of us with something to defend us in time of real need. I quietly said to myself, 'If it means death, then it is death. I must face it like a man.' I faced the disagreeable fact of my possible death before the next harvest.

'Yes, I hear you, father,' I said, turning to the man. 'I die before the next harvest, but you won't see your family tonight. I'm sorry you did not bid them farewell. They will never see you again.'

'What!' he cried, sneering at me. 'How can a kid like you know such deep things of life?'

'Do you think I was born of a tree? I have a father, a grandfather, and a chain of ancestors. I die before the next harvest and you today.'

'I was just playing, my boy.'

'No playing. You are a man; you have spoken. I am a man; I have spoken. What men have spoken can't be unspoken.'

Silence and stillness fell upon him and I emerged the master of the situation. He was gradually becoming the victim of the situation he had created.

'Forgive me, son of Sithole,' he pleaded.

After many pretended refusals I forgave him and told him to go home.

'I can't go home alone now, son of Sithole. It's getting dark. Accompany me, please,' he said.

I went into my bedroom and got my black walking-stick and then I led the way along a narrow winding path and he followed behind. With my walking-stick I hit the darkness right and left. 'No, boys, don't seize the man. He's our friend.' As I said this I ran behind him and chased away my imaginary boys, giving them a good talking-to. For two miles the poor man was silent with fear and I spoke again and again to my imaginary spooks.

He believed without any shadow of doubt that I was a witch-doctor and that I possessed many evil spirits in the forest. This greatly improved school and church attendance!

When I was transferred to Dadaya Mission to teach Standard Five there, I found that many teachers were very keen to do private studies. Mr. Todd volunteered to take them in some subjects and I also volunteered to take them in others. They were very keen in their lessons. Side by side with my teaching work I also read for my Matriculation Exemption Certificate. I would have saved money to go for my university training, but I had three sisters to educate, so I had to content myself with private study.

In 1946 I got married, and 1947 brought us a baby girl and some real domestic trouble. My mother insisted that we smoke the baby, and I refused. I told her that since I was a Christian and an educated man I could not do that. Then she would count on her fingers some outstanding Christians and educated people who smoked their children and tied *intebe* round their waists. She argued that unless the baby was treated by the witch-doctors she would die. Finally, she told me that with or without my consent she would smoke the child and call in a local witch-doctor to treat the baby.

'You can't do things like that with my baby, mother,' I protested.

'That's not your baby. The baby belongs to the whole Sithole family. When you were born I smoked you. All your sisters and brothers were smoked. I have now nine children all smoked. No baby ever lives unless it is smoked.'

She had the support of almost everyone, but I insisted that no such thing was going to be done to the baby. Canaan, my wife, was inclined to listen to the voice of experience rather than to that of a newcomer in matrimony.

I rudely said to both my mother and my mother-in-law, 'We didn't plan that the baby was going to be female or to be what she is. Someone did that. The same person will continue to look after the baby. I had no voice in my own creation.'

My mother-in-law remarked, 'My son, you have wonderful faith.'

'It's not faith,' retorted my mother sourly, 'it's childishness.'

1948 found me at Tegwane Training Institution, where I was employed as an assistant method master to Miss Dora Warwick, who was the method mistress and Headmistress of the Teacher Training Department. I learnt many things from Miss Warwick. Her great energies well fitted her for the hard task of dealing with all kinds of boys and girls who were training as teachers.

I went through a course of Bible study, after which I became an accredited local preacher of the British Methodist Church. I attended regularly the local Y.M.C.U. group and my eyes were opened to the great desire among boys and girls to preach the Gospel and testify. I enjoyed preaching at the Plumtree jail. I had never done this before, and it had never occurred to my mind that people in jail were worth preaching to. There was something in the prisoners' singing which deeply touched me. I was left in no doubt that most of them were not beyond the point of redemption. I became engrossed in preaching to them. Despite the austere atmosphere of the prison-cells, the prisoners had not lost their sense of humour.

The Rev. Mr. Chapman said one day, 'Brother, what about the ministry?' And as usual I tried to evade the question. My cousin, the Rev. O. D. Ramushu, said to me another day, 'Why don't you join the ministry?' As usual I hesitated to make a reply. Then he went on in his blunt way, 'You fear there's not much in the ministry, eh?' I was interested in the ministry but something held me back.

At the end of 1950 I left Tegwane and joined a newly organized church. I now had an opportunity of preaching. For the first time in my life I saw with my own eyes how Gospel-starved the people were in the rural areas away from mission stations. Great crowds came if they heard that I was going to preach to them. People were interested in studying the simple word of God in the Bible. We had fewer workers, but more people to preach to. I had never ridden a bicycle so much before. I was on my 'Gospel bicycle' nearly every week-end after classes on Friday for places between ten and twenty-five miles away from my school. I did this for two years. The Rev-E. T. J. Nemapare tried to make arrangements for me to train as a minister, but owing to financial difficulties he could not. Soon the poor financial circumstances of the young church made it very difficult for both my wife and me to continue our services there.

We joined the Mount Selinda teaching staff in 1953. The first sermon I preached at Mount Selinda made a good impression, and ever after the Rev. Frank Meacham used to say to me, 'Ndabaningi, you are not a teacher. Your place is in the ministry. I am not joking. I mean it.'

I must mention here some of my inner struggles with regard to God's work. Although I started preaching at the age of 18, I did not think of taking up preaching as full-time service. I always argued with my disturbing soul that I was a teacher by profession, and that preaching was all right for me as a part-time job. Many a time I had felt something stirring my conscience, but I dreaded to make the move. Sometimes I thought it was older people's work. But all these were excuses to soothe my troubled conscience. This struggle continued well over eight years. To be or not to be a full-time worker for Christ worried me; Canaan said to me one day, as we sat discussing the question, 'If God intends you for full-time worker, don't worry about deciding now. We can't vote on the matter today. He'll work out His way for you.' I dismissed the matter for the next four years although the thing kept on coming back to me from time to time. I had decided to evade the call by being silent about it. I contented myself with teaching as my full-time job and preaching as part-time.

One evening I mentioned again the matter to Canaan. 'Yes, I know the thing is always worrying you. It's there, I can see.'

'But I can't go and train as a minister now. We've three children.' I tried to excuse my reluctance about obeying the call.

'You looked after Phike while I went for training as a school-teacher,' said Canaan. 'It's my turn now to look after the children while you go for training as a minister.'

'Three years!' I cried.

'Why not? I know you'll never be happy until you satisfy this thing in you. When we got married I found you talking about it. It's seven years now since then and you are still talking about it.'

We invited Miss Lindile Nyembezi to our house one evening.

She was one of the old Zulu missionaries who had come to Gazaland for the spreading of Christ's Gospel. I told her the story of my troubles. For a long time she prayed and kept on repeating, 'Show him the way.... If it is monetary consideration holding him back ... good Lord, show him the way. If it is an anticipated evil that makes him not surrender himself to Thee ... good Lord, show him the way.'

Then Canaan prayed. I had never heard her pray like that before. 'If it is Thy will, Lord, that he give all his time for Thee, help him to decide.' At times she was overcome with weeping. The whole atmosphere was tense.

After Canaan and Miss Nyembezi had prayed the three of us sat in silence for some time.

I felt greatly strengthened. I decided to see our local minister, the Rev. Elija Mwadira. I told him about my strong call to the Christian ministry, and I expressed the view that I feared to make any formal application to the Church as I was a new man at the place and that after three or four years I would make one.

'If the call is there,' said the Rev. Mr. Mwadira, 'make it now. Say it so that we know it is there.' After a long prayer he advised me to go and see the Rev. John Heinrich in connexion with my call.

Following the Rev. Mr. Mwadira's advice, I went to see both the Rev. Mrs. Heinrich and the Rev. J. Heinrich. They were interested in my story, and the Rev. Mr. Heinrich solemnly said, 'I am convinced of your Christian conviction. We have sensed that since you came here.' He advised me as to the proper procedure. Both Mr. and Mrs. Heinrich prayed.

After this I went to Miss Ivy Craig, a very close friend of mine who regarded me as her son and our children as her grandchildren. I told her. She was touched, and she simply said, 'We have been praying for such things.' She started an evening Bible discussion group which broadened my Christian outlook and deepened my Christian experience. Like Mr. and Mrs. Heinrich she always endeavoured to surround me with Christian literature.

The only thing that remained now was to make my application to the Church Association and the Mission Council. I drafted the application and called Miss Nyembezi and Canaan. I read it to them. Miss Nyembezi prayed fervently and wept. Then Canaan prayed and also wept. I could feel that these women had completely surrendered themselves to God. There was something better felt than expressed in words. 'If the thing worrying you, my son,' said Miss Nyembezi, 'is of God, then He'll answer you.'

I duly dispatched the application to the Superintendent of Churches and I received the following reply:

Dear Mr. Sithole,

... I wish to thank you for this letter. It is inspiring to receive such a letter, and one does not receive this kind of letter very often.

We are grateful to God who has placed this desire within your heart, and know that He will guide you and us as we give your request most sympathetic and thoughtful consideration.

May God be very near to you and give His own guidance for the future as to what is best for you and the Mission here. I personally hope that it will be possible for you to take theological training and serve Christ in this Field in the years to come.

John Marsh
Superintendent of Churches

A meeting of the Church Association was held at the end of the year. My application was presented, and Mr. E. J. Mlambo, the devoted worker for the welfare of the public, regarded the application as the answer to their long prayers. 'At last God has answered us,' he said. The application was unanimously accepted. The Mission Council, which was the supreme body of the American Board Mission of Southern Rhodesia, unanimously approved of the application.

A sermon I had preached at Mount Selinda Institute on 'Our need of love and not weapons' was sent by Miss Craig to the Secretary for Africa, of the American Board, Boston. This was at the time of race trouble in Durban. She thought the Secretary might like such material to counteract adverse conceptions in the minds of people in America. The result was that it kindled an interest and opened the way for study in America.

CHAPTER 2

Studying in the United States

We left Port Beira, Mozambique, on 18 January 1955. The *Braemar Castle* had about a thousand people on board including the crew. I had never travelled by boat before, and naturally I had my fears as the vessel floated on the vast Indian Ocean where I could see neither land nor any other vessel around. In spite of my fears, however, I took courage in the knowledge that there were so many people, so that if anything went wrong with the boat I would not die alone. I would be in the good company of fellow-diers. Big numbers are reassuring and give a sense of security.

The *Braemar Castle* coursed along the east coast of Africa and called at Dar-es-Salaam, Zanzibar, Mombasa, Aden, and Port Said. At Aden I had the satisfaction of having a camel ride. All these places which had been to me geographical and historical names seemed to put on flesh and I relived some of my history lessons. Our next stop, after ploughing through the blue sparkling waters of the Mediterranean Sea, was Genoa, the native city of Christopher Columbus, who discovered America in 1492. We visited his town and saw the house in which he was born. From Genoa we travelled by train to Florence, the home of the Renaissance and the former capital of Tuscany. We spent two days there. The architecture, art, and sculpture of the Renaissance seemed to breathe from many parts of the ancient and yet modern city. From Florence we went to Rome where we spent a week sight-seeing. We visited the Vatican City and I was thrilled when I entered St. Peter's Cathedral. Our visit to the Roman Forum brought back to life the voices of Julius Caesar, Mark Antony, Brutus, and others. I thought at one time I could hear the voices of bygone days:

Mark Antony: Friends, Romans, Countrymen, lend me your ears; I come to bury Caesar, not to praise him. . . .

. . . .

You all did love him once,—not without cause:
What cause withholds you, then, to mourn for him?
O judgement, thou art fled to brutish beasts,
And men have lost their reason! . . .

The crowds of tourists seemed to be saying:

The will, the will! we will hear Caesar's will.

From Rome we went to Naples, where we spent another week of sight-seeing. From Naples we boarded an American boat—the *Constitution*—which touched at Genoa where we collected most of our luggage, which we had left there. At the Azores I ran into great difficulty. The sea was choppy. I was sick for two days. I lost my appetite. At times I regretted that I had left home, and my missionary friends had quite some amusement.

'You don't seem to enjoy your trip, Ndaba,' said the Rev. John Marsh who was returning to the United States after he and his wife Dorothy Marsh had served as missionaries in Southern Rhodesia for fifteen years.

'I'll never travel like this again,' I vowed.

In our company were Mr. and Mrs. Marsh; Miss Ivy Craig, who had served as a missionary in Southern Rhodesia for thirty-four years; Miss Theresa Buck, a medical missionary who was going on furlough; and the two Marsh children—Louise and John. They were all greatly excited as the *Constitution* neared New York Harbour. In spite of their age and serious dispositions, the Statue of Liberty excited them like a group of young students. The Italians who were visiting the States for the first time shed tears at the sight of the Statue of Liberty. For my part I did not know what it was all about, but I was impressed by the fact that people love their country like mad. It is the only spot on earth they call their own.

It was on 8 March that we docked at New York Harbour. It was wonderful to be on land again. I was now in the United States. I was going to remain in this country for the next four years I was not going to see my four children and wife for that period. I had entered the United States not on a student's visa but on an immigrant's visa. In other words, I could take out American citizenship if I desired to in the future. We spent three days in New York City before proceeding to Boston where I was to study. When we got to Boston I was despatched to the Walker Missionary Home, Auburndale—eight miles outside Boston. The Walker Missionary Home was certainly a cross-roads of missionaries. I met missionaries from Angola, Ghana, India, China, South Africa, Ceylon, East Africa, and so on.

I had five months to myself before I was to begin my theological studies at the Andover-Newton Theological Seminary, Massachusetts, which was about six miles away from the Walker Missionary Home. During the first five months I did some speaking for the then American Board of Commissioners for Foreign Missions, now the United Church Board for World Ministries. This was an excellent orientation period, and Dr. John Reuling, who was then the Board's Secretary for Africa, and who spoke Zulu fairly well since he had been Principal at Adams College, Natal, South Africa, saw to it that I was sent to the various Church groups in the various States. It was the first time that I felt white people treated me like a real human being. Back home I had been made to feel that I was less than a human being. The three and a half years I spent in the United States were amongst the happiest years of my life, although I was reminded of the colour bar back home when I visited the Deep South. Yes, racialism in the Deep South was deep, deep, deep. It greeted me everywhere. But in New England and the Mid-West I never encountered the Monster of Racialism. During the summer of 1955 I worked in the various junior high and senior high school camps where I met thousands of American boys and girls who were eager to listen to stories from Africa. I also worked in adult camps where I met men and women from various walks of life. As a result of this deputation work for the American Board of Commissioners for Foreign Missions I was able to visit over thirty different States during my stay in America.

I began my theological studies in September 1955. There were over four hundred students. It would be outside the scope of this book if I went into the details of my happy and very useful stay at the Andover-Newton Theological Seminary. The professors there greatly inspired me. I was particularly inspired by Professor John Brush who taught us Church History, and under whose guidance I did my dissertation 'The Causes of the Reformation', for which I finally received my degree of Bachelor of Divinity in June 1958. I also did clinical training at the Boston City Hospital where I came face to face with the ugly facts of death, dying, and hovering between life and death. I had been used to seeing dead black men but not dead white men. I had been used to seeing ill black men but not ill white men. For six months, along with others, I was taught the art of ministering physically and spiritually to the sick. In spite of the rigours of the training I still feel that that training strengthened my deep belief in the oneness of mankind the world over. Man's sufferings, anxieties, sense of guilt, destinies, and the like are more or less the same.

Towards the end of 1956, my wife Canaan joined me in the States. Some of the Church groups I had visited had collected money for her air fare. It was a happy reunion after a separation of fifteen months. We lived together on the campus and we were, accommodation-wise, classified as a 'childless couple'. After twelve months my wife had to return home to take care of our four children, the oldest of whom—Siphikeleho—is now doing her B.A. course at Barnard College, New York.

During my second and third years I worked as a Sunday School teacher and as an assistant pastor, and I treasure this practical experience of coming into contact with men and women, and boys and girls. I found the American people very friendly, outgoing, large-hearted, and tending to overreach themselves. I felt quite at home with most of them. Their standard of measure is success. They do not measure people by their descent or their families, but by their success, although a handful of them still measure their importance by the *Mayflower* which brought their forefathers to America in 1620. To the average American, it is not the beginning that counts, but the achievement. A man has to achieve something to count among his fellow-men. As they say there, 'You begin as a nothing. That's nothing. You end up as a something. That's something.' This is their way of saying there's nothing wrong with starting from nothing. What matters is that a man builds or achieves something from nothing!

One of my exciting experiences while studying in the United States was when my wife and I visited the State of Montana, where we worked in adult summer camps as counsellors and guest speakers. While we were in Southern Rhodesia we had heard so much about the cowboys of the Mid-West. We closely inquired into their whereabouts and some of our American friends made arrangements for us to go and live on a ranch for a week. We were greatly excited at the idea of seeing real cowboys. We went to one ranch owned by a man obviously over forty. He had a good team of horses, more than ten of them. He took us to a nearby rodeo. There the cowboys were in full swing. They were riding wild, tossing horses on whose backs had never sat a human being before. Some fell off and left the rodeo limping, but others stuck to the horses' backs until the horses got adjusted to being sat upon by human beings. To our surprise, there was our good host on one of these wild, tossing horses. His performance was superb. After the show I said to him, 'I thought you were fifty!'

'No, only forty-eight,' he answered simply. 'Why?'

'Riding a wild horse like that at forty-eight!' I cried.

'Oh, no. I feel so much younger whenever I am on a horse. The horse is right inside me,' he said, and he seemed to take on a new lease of life. He was animation itself. Back at home he would have gone down for a man who has *shavi rebiza*, i.e. is possessed of the spirit of a horse.

The following morning he dressed me up like a real cowboy—big felt hat, large scarf, black cowboy shirt, and a pair of large cowboy trousers. There I was, a perfect black cowboy who had never ridden a horse before, although I had ridden on oxen and donkeys. I mounted one of his white horses in fear and trembling, but put on a bold front for Canaan who made a photographic record of the whole incident. My host and I spent two hours on horseback, but I did not like the aftermath the following morning!

When Canaan returned home in 1957, she showed to our church leaders some of these pictures she had taken while I was dressed up like a cowboy. They were shocked! They complained, 'We sent him to the States to learn to be a Minister of Religion, not to be a cowboy.' The impression my cowboy pictures made was that I was spending most of my time in the American rodeos! They strongly felt it was below the dignity of a Minister of Religion to play a cowboy!

Towards the end of 1957 I started on my dissertation 'The Causes of the Reformation'. My whole contention was briefly this, that the real cause of the Reformation is to be sought in the nature of the Christian substance, which requires interpretation, which in turn is not infallible. Wherever human beings engage in interpretative work conflict is inevitable. This is not only true in religious matters, but in other matters as well. Capitalists are always at each other's throats when they start interpreting capitalism. Socialists cross swords in their interpretation of Marxism. What finally took place in the sixteenth century, which history has come to regard as the Reformation, was caused by the natural human need for interpretation of the *Christian substance* which was deposited in the hands of the first disciples of Jesus in the first century.

In June 1958, I graduated, and I went to the Immigration Office to present myself for departure from the United States.

'Why, man,' cried the immigration official. 'This is an immigrant's visa. You can now become a citizen of the United States if you like to.'

'I'm aware of that,' I said, 'but I must go home.'

'But don't you like it here?' he cried.

'I like it very much.'

'You see, you have now been in this country for almost four years. You are not treated as a student who must return on completion of his course of study. You are treated as an immigrant. This is very important for you.'

'In a way you're right,' I said, 'but I must return home.'

'You are not free in your country, are you?' he asked, trying to knock some sense into my head.

'That's why I must return home,' I said.

'To be unfree?' he asked, his eyes growing bigger.

'To free my country,' I said simply.

'I see. Good luck to you, fellow.'

As I sit in my indefinite detention I sometimes wonder what my American friend would say if he came here and found me in detention. Wouldn't he say, 'If only you had taken my advice you wouldn't be in this mess,' and he would be right from his point of view. But I would also remind him, 'I told you I wanted to free my country, and this is how it's done,' and I would also be right from my point of view.

CHAPTER 3

Entering Nationalist Politics

When I returned to Southern Rhodesia in June 1958 after spending three and a half years at the Andover-Newton Theological Seminary and having obtained my degree, I was naturally happy to be back home. I had had a wonderful time in the United States from 1955 to 1958, but there is nothing like home. The language, the song, the dance, and the people of Zimbabwe were a part of me. It was once again refreshing to eat the *sadza* of Zimbabwe which had built my physical self from childhood to manhood.

I found the entire atmosphere highly charged with explosive African nationalist politics. The Southern Rhodesia African National Congress was just beginning to make a real impression on the African population. People were now talking of majority rule. The air was supercharged with 'one man one vote'. Detectives were trailing African nationalists from sunrise to sunset, and sometimes after sunset.

I was appointed Principal of Chikore Central Primary School at the beginning of 1959. I was keenly interested in participating in current affairs. I felt I should use my pen to put across the African cause. I therefore became a regular contributor to Rhodesia's local papers. The African Education Department was not too happy with my political articles, but they did not formally express their dislike, and I went ahead. But no African teacher was allowed by the African Education Department to participate actively in politics. That is to say, no teacher was allowed to hold an executive position in any political party. The effect of this was to deprive the African nationalist movement of really educated people. It would appear that the African Education Department used the question of a relatively high salary to frighten African teachers off politics, since if any one of them actively participated in politics he would lose his teaching post and thus his high salary. African nationalist politics at that time were regarded as a poor man's occupation.

On 29 February 1959, came my biggest shock. The Southern Rhodesia African National Congress was banned, and over 500 national, provincial, and district branch leaders were bundled up during 'Operation Dawn' and whisked away from their homes to jail, where they were detained, some for a few months, others for many months, and still others restricted for four years. I had had great hopes of the A.N.C. I had been in the process of setting up branches in Chipinga district. But now the whole plan dried up in my hands! I had got official receipt books and other official books from George Nyandoro, the Secretary-General, and Robert Chikerama, the Vice-President. The excuse given for the ban was that the A.N.C. had a plot to kill white people in Rhodesia. Nothing could have been more incredible to me. There were rumours that I was also going to be collected in view of my political articles, but of course this never happened. One thing that remained clear to me was that the white man was determined to destroy the African nationalist movement. The white man was simply determined to see white supremacy in the saddle for all time.

On 1 January 1960, the National Democratic Party rose on the ruins of the African National Congress. I was greatly excited, and I made several trips to Salisbury to discuss matters with the national leaders of the new party. Michael Mawema, its interim President, and the other members of the committee, were very helpful and from time to time they let me into their confidence.

Towards Easter, 1960, I was scheduled to deliver a lecture at the University College of Rhodesia and Nyasaland. This was to be on a Sunday night. My lecture was to be on 'Christian Love in Human Relations'. I got to Salisbury on Sunday morning, and I found my old friend Leopold Takawira waiting for me at the railway station. 'You see, Ndaba, in an hour's time, an N.D.P. rally will be held in the Stordat Hall. People would like you to conduct devotions for them.' Naturally, I accepted the invitation. What better opportunity could a Minister of Religion have than one like this ?

We drove to Stordat Hall. It was packed to capacity—over 1,000 people inside and many outside. I chose for my text 'God Created Man'. The reception was warm and reverent. Then speaker after speaker delivered speech after speech until they went through the list. Then, without consulting me, Messrs. Michael Mawema, Takawira, Morton Malianga, and others decided to call upon me to speak. They knew that the position I held (since January, 1960) at Mount Selinda Institute did not allow me to make any political speeches. But they chose to ignore this. There was something higher than a departmental regulation.

'Ladies and Gentlemen,' Mr. Takawira addressed the gathering, 'you have all heard the Reverend Ndabaningi Sithole speak to us as our Minister of Religion. Now we would like to hear him speak to us as an African nationalist. His book *African Nationalism* is now our nationalist Bible.'

The people went mad with cheers. Some held up copies of *African Nationalism*, which had been first published in June 1959. 'The author of *African Nationalism*!' they shouted, and again they cheered and stood on their feet.

That was the first time I realized I was going to deliver a political speech. In Africa we do not speak from papers. We speak from the heart. If the thing is not in the heart, you do not speak. If it is there, why, you do. I had my heart, and the thing—African freedom—was in it, and so I rose to my feet in the midst of deafening cheers. I delivered my speech for thirty minutes. In it I reminded the people that Zimbabwe was our country; that it was important we organized ourselves throughout the country as efficiently as we could; that other independent African countries won their independence because they worked unflinchingly for it; and that we also would get our independence if we fought with the consuming zeal of freedom fighters.

I sat down amid deafening cheers. The speech, apparently, had gone down very well with the people. They waved *African Nationalism* as if to say, 'That's the stuff we want to hear.'

In the evening I went to deliver my lecture at the University College. Quite a good number of nationalists came to hear it, and as it was a public lecture, they were allowed in. At 10 p.m. Leopold Takawira drove me back to Mount Selinda—a distance of 271 miles. We got home at 4 a.m.

Two days after my political speech, I got a phone message that I was required to be in Salisbury on Wednesday to see the African Education Department. I knew instinctively that my speech had not gone down too well with the Education Department! At 2 p.m. I appeared before the Director of African Education, his Assistant, the Chief Magistrate, and Mr. G. Grant, the Field Secretary of the United Church in Rhodesia. The Director handed over an account of my speech to the Chief Magistrate to read and decide if it was political. He ran through it and returned the verdict 'Highly political'.

'Now, Mr. Sithole, you as the President of the African Teachers' Association of Southern Rhodesia should have known better that you are not allowed to make any political speeches,' the Director reminded me. 'Why did you do such a thing?'

'I've nothing to say,' I said. 'I am completely at your mercy in terms of your rules. Do as you please.'

I was asked to make an undertaking that I was not going to do anything like that in future. I said I was still going to think about it. I returned to Mount Selinda. There was no question of choosing between fighting for the freedom of my country and my high salary. Freedom came first. 'We must be treated like men in our country,' I quietly said to myself as I turned the matter in my mind.

In October 1960 the first national elections of the National Democratic Party were held, and I was elected Treasurer-General. This infuriated the Director of African Education and he terminated my teaching services by a telegram. I was advised to make representations, but I ignored the suggestion. I accepted fully the logic of my own political actions. My sympathetic friends anxiously asked, 'How are you now going to live since the Education Department is no longer going to pay you a penny?' To this I jocularly answered, 'We lived long before the Education Department was born, and we'll continue to live long after it is dead and forgotten.'

Now that I was a free man I threw in my lot with my colleagues on the National Executive. At the beginning of 1961, we moved from our mission house at Mount Selinda to our 'Freedom Farm' which was only two miles away from Mount Selinda. Canaan, my wife, ran a small retail shop at the Chako African Township. The National Democratic Party grew from strength to strength, and I thoroughly enjoyed myself playing my small part in this nationalist movement, but in December 1962 the Party was banned and all its funds and vehicles confiscated by the Government. During the same month, we formed the Zimbabwe African People's Union. Mr. Joshua Nkomo, who had been elected President of the N.D.P. in October 1960, was the interim President of the new Party for which I became the National Chairman. Again, the new Party which had risen on the ruins of the N.D.P. grew like a wild fire.

Among my duties as National Chairman, was one of explaining the policies of the Party. I spent a lot of time writing articles and addressing influential house-to-house meetings, which opened my eyes as nothing else could have done. Most European liberals, I discovered, while in full sympathy with the miserable lot of the African people, approached the problem as one of the white man ruling the African justly, not one of Africans taking over from the whites. The latter was our approach. They wanted to see the black man treated justly as a human being. They wanted him to receive a fair economic reward based on merit and qualifications, and not on the colour of his skin. They wanted to see the African allowed to use public facilities like anybody else. They wanted to see universal education provided for the African child and a host of other improvements made for the African. But they had serious reservations on an African take-over. They did not subscribe to 'one man one vote'.

In September 1962 I went to Athens in Greece, where I attended the Fourth International Conference on World Politics and presented a written paper on the current problems of Southern Rhodesia. This conference had been sponsored by Western scholars, but it was not attended by any scholars from the Eastern bloc. It lasted for four days and the experience was most uplifting. On the morning of the break-up of the Conference, I received news that our Party—the Zimbabwe African People's Union—had been banned by Sir Edgar Whitehead's Government. It left me with a most horrible feeling. It was difficult to know what to do on the spur of the moment. I decided to fly to Cairo where I met our representative, who was also equally worried about the banning of our Party. After a week I flew to Dar-es-Salaam where I found Mr. Joshua Nkomo waiting for me. After discussing the situation, we decided that he return home, and I remain outside the country and carry on the activities of our nationalist movement. I did not quite like the idea of remaining outside my country, but I had to, as a matter of duty. By disposition I do not get much fun outside my country.

In Tanganyika I settled down to the task of advancing our nationalist cause. Among other things I broadcast to Southern Rhodesia once a week, and I also visited the Congo (Kinshasa) and Congo (Brazzaville), Ethiopia, the United Arab Republic, Belgium, the United Kingdom, and the United States. I appeared before the Committee of Twenty-Four and petitioned there the African cause. On two occasions I met Mr. R. A. Butler, the then Secretary for Central Africa, with regard to the African cause in Southern Rhodesia. I also had the opportunity to visit Israel, and as a student of the Holy Bible and a Christian Minister of Religion I was greatly interested in visiting the various biblical places. Mrs. Golda Meir, Israel's Minister for Foreign Affairs, made it possible for me to visit many of these places.

Towards the end of January 1963 I had a surprise visit from Canaan, my wife, after a period of almost five months. Together we attended the Afro-Asian Conference held at Moshi, Tanganyika, towards the end of February. I led the Zimbabwe delegation. It was quite an uplifting experience meeting so many African nationalists from all over Africa and delegates from independent African countries, from communist China, Russia, and other socialist countries. It was quite a treat to listen to many of their speeches. I also had the opportunity of delivering a twenty-five-minute speech to the representatives of 65 countries assembled there. When I ended my greatly cheered speech with, 'In Zimbabwe we are engaged in a bitter struggle to destroy the government of the white settlers, by the white settlers, for the white settlers, so that it is replaced by the government of the people, by the people, for the people,' deafening cheers went up, and many delegates, and in particular the PAFMECSA delegates, felt very proud of the speech. From a personal point of view, it gave me a new place in the hearts of many people who were present.

In April 1963 I went to Addis Ababa to attend a summit conference of the Heads of African States. I joined Mr. Joshua Nkomo and the rest of the members of our National Executive of the banned Zimbabwe African People's Union (ZAPU). They had run out of the country *en bloc* on the advice and insistence of President Joshua Nkomo. They had thought the nationalist struggle could be better served in this manner. We had very sharp disagreement among ourselves. Some of us felt very strongly that 'run-away politics' were not going to emancipate Zimbabwe. We felt we must all return home and face the music. Although this summit conference had many good things to learn from, our hearts were galled by the fact that the entire executive of ZAPU had fled from the country!

After the conference we returned to Dar-es-Salaam bitterly divided among ourselves. At last Mr. Joshua Nkomo, our President, was forced to return home to be with our followers, but the whole thing had left a sour taste in our mouths. In June we split into two— the Sithole group and the Nkomo group. The people at home were also divided accordingly. I had to return home immediately. Meanwhile I received cuttings from Rhodesian papers in which the police were alleged to have made a statement that if I returned home I would face a charge with a maximum sentence of imprisonment for twenty years without an option of a fine. The charge arose out of the broadcasts I made to Southern Rhodesia from Dar-es-Salaam. Messrs. Leopold Takawira, Robert Mugabe, and Morton Malianga and I vowed that whatever charges we faced at home, it was our duty to go back and face them. And so we returned home, though not all at the same time.

I returned home on 28 July 1963. At the Salisbury Airport I was arrested and served with the charge-sheet. I was relieved to note that the maximum sentence I was facing was only five years, and not twenty years as had been suggested in the local papers. A clear net profit of fifteen years! That was not bad business. I slept in the police cells, but I was perfectly happy to be back home after an absence of eleven months from home. The next morning I appeared in court and I was formally charged and remanded out of custody on bail of £100 and on condition that I reported to the police twice a week. The charge arose out of a circular I had written while I was in Dar-es-Salaam and circulated to people in Southern Rhodesia urging voters to boycott the December 1962 elections.

The presiding magistrate found me guilty, and before pronouncing sentence he asked me if I had anything to say in mitigation. I told him, 'I am not sorry for anything I wrote in that circular; I still consider it my duty to correct the government I sincerely believe to be oppressive.'

I was sentenced to twelve months' imprisonment with hard labour, and without option of a fine. We lodged an appeal to the Appellate Division of the High Court of Southern Rhodesia which we lost after seven months. I served the twelve-months jail sentence in the Salisbury Central Prison from 1964 to 1965. When I finished serving this sentence, I was served with a five-year restriction order from 19 May 1965 to 18 May 1970.

In my restriction area—Sikombela—I and my colleagues were haunted by the serious threat of the white-settler Government seizing independence unilaterally. On 15 October I and my colleagues decided to write to the Attorney-General of Southern Rhodesia regarding this matter of U.D.I. (unilateral declaration of independence).

Nine of us[1] signed the letter in which we asked that sixteen members of the Cabinet, including the Prime Minister, be prosecuted. If the Attorney-General declined to prosecute 'at our instance

[1] The people who signed this letter were: Ndabaningi Sithole (President, ZANU), Leopold Takawira (Deputy President), Robert Mugabe (Secretary-General), Edson Zvobgo (Deputy Secretary-General), Enos Nkala (Treasurer-General), Michael Mawema (National Organizing Secretary), Morton Malianga (Secretary for Youth), Simon Muzenda (Deputy National Organizing Secretary), and Edgar Tekere (Deputy Secretary for Youth).

as a section of the public' we applied at the same time 'for a group licence authorizing us to institute private prosecutions'. We alleged that the sixteen people were guilty, first of high treason in that they advocated unilateral declaration of independence, and secondly, of planning the overthrow of the Southern Rhodesia (Constitution) Order in Council, 1961, which was not only in contravention of parts of both the Preservation of Constitutional Government Act and of the Law and Order (Maintenance) Act but also of Section ix of the Constitution.

We stated that as a result of these offences we might find ourselves citizens under an illegal government, that any contravention of the Southern Rhodesia (Constitution) Order in Council might destroy 'guarantees regarding civil liberty, citizenship and membership of the Commonwealth', and that any unilateral declaration of independence would place us and 'the general citizenry in the position of rebels against Her Majesty Queen Elizabeth II and liable whenever we enter British territory anywhere in the world to prosecution for high treason'.

We declared our intention of applying to the High Court for a licence to prosecute if the Attorney-General declined to do so; and we sent copies of the letter to the Governor of Southern Rhodesia, Sir Humphrey Gibbs, and to the British High Commissioner, Mr. J. B. Johnston, resident in Salisbury.

Because of the threat of a unilateral declaration of independence, the British Prime Minister, Mr. Harold Wilson, and a staff of fifty came to Southern Rhodesia on 25 October 1965, with the expressed intention of averting the threatened unilateral declaration of independence by the Southern Rhodesian Government which is predominantly a white-settler Government. Our official delegation of eleven people went from restriction to Salisbury to see the British Premier.[2] We presented a memorandum dated 25 October—signed by me—to the British Prime Minister.

We asked the British Government to exercise its legal and constitutional powers and responsibility in Rhodesia. We pointed out that the 1961 Constitution was unacceptable to the African people of Rhodesia and that the white minority Government had rendered it impossible for Africans to express opinions without fear of restriction or imprisonment. We protested that we had not been consulted in discussions between the British and Rhodesian Governments, and

[2] The eleven people were the nine who had signed the letter (footnote p. 36) together with Advocate Edson Sithole and Dr. Elisha Mutasa.

stressed that the point at issue was a new constitution for Southern Rhodesia which should be the result of a conference held between the Rhodesian Government and the Nationalists under the chairmanship of the British Government. Such a conference should be held immediately and the issue of unilateral declaration of independence treated as the red herring we considered it to be. We pointed out that in our opinion the British Government's weak handling of the constitutional crisis, exemplified by the test cases of the withdrawal of the Union Jack from Southern Rhodesia's Pretoria office and the appointment of her own ambassador in Lisbon, was the cause of the present impasse. It looked as though Britain intended to hand over independence to a minority, and not, as had been British colonial policy hitherto, to a majority government. We asked the British Government to call a constitutional conference to include representatives of all interested parties and to aim at majority rule based on 'one man one vote'. Thereafter, independence should be granted. Should the present Rhodesian Government not co-operate, we asked the British Government to suspend the 1961 Constitution and to impose majority rule.

In an addendum to this document we went more fully into the matter of the discussions between the British and Rhodesian Governments during which a five-point formula for progress towards independence had been offered to Rhodesia. We rejected this formula *in toto* because it did not provide for majority rule before independence. For the same reason we rejected the idea of Britain's proposed promise to guarantee African subjects of Rhodesia from oppression and injustice while steps towards majority rule were being made. If the British Government was even now hesitating to send troops to Rhodesia to protect her African subjects from a threatened act of high treason, we asked, how much more would she hesitate after independence had been granted?

We scorned, before the British Prime Minister, the suggestion that independence should be granted to the white-settler Government after a treaty had been gone into by the Rhodesian Government and the British Government guaranteeing majority rule after white-settler independence. We pointed out in unequivocal terms, 'At present there are constitutional arrangements which Mr. Smith is threatening with a unilateral declaration of independence, and the British Government is finding it impossible to stop him. What guarantee, on the one hand, have we that Mr. Smith who is at present defying the present constitutional arrangements will respect the provisions of the proposed treaty? On the other hand, what guarantee have we to suppose that the British Government which is at present failing to make Mr. Smith honour the present constitutional arrangements, will be able to enforce the provisions of the treaty in the event of Mr. Smith dishonouring them?' We killed the whole idea on the same day that the British Attorney-General had arrived in Salisbury to work on it. The Rhodesian Premier, Mr. Ian Smith, had agreed to the idea of a treaty. We presented our formula simply and clearly: No independence before majority rule. First, majority rule, then independence.

We returned to Sikombela Restriction under strong armed police guard. On 5 November 1965, Mr. Ian Smith declared a state of emergency throughout the country and most leading African nationalists in restriction and outside restriction were moved into detention and placed under strong armed police guard. On 11 November 1965 Mr. Ian Smith seized independence unilaterally. I revised my book *African Nationalism* while in detention.

CHAPTER 4

More Legal Battles

Perhaps, to complete this autobiographical sketch, and to show the difficulties under which African nationalists carry on their work of establishing freedom and independence in their native lands, I had better describe some of my political activities which resulted in fifty-one charges against me between 30 July 1963 and 22 June 1964.

After I returned to Southern Rhodesia, my group was very keen to form a new political party since there was none since the banning of the Zimbabwe African People's Union in September 1962. On 8 August 1963 we formed the Zimbabwe African National Union. This greatly antagonized the Nkomo group, later to form themselves into the People's Caretaker Council. Notorious inter-party clashes took place time and again. As President of ZANU the police kept me under close observation. My house was raided from time to time. The privacy of our home at Highfields was at the mercy of the police who seemed to take particular delight in embarrassing and humiliating us by such acts. The National Headquarters of the Party, which were at Vanguard House, Railway Avenue, Salisbury, were often raided by the police, who left everything turned upside down. But we carried on as best we could. From 22 to 24 May, we held our inaugural conference and I was elected unanimously the President of ZANU by delegates who numbered nearly a thousand.

To return to my legal battles: I was accused of entering tribal trust land and remaining there in contravention of a 1961 order barring me from entering any such land where more than three million Africans lived. I defended myself by explaining that I had told the police I was going to enter a township and that the 1961 banning order did not bar me from this. The District Commissioner admitted that the terminology and description of African areas ('Townships', 'Business Centres', etc.) was not clear, and I was acquitted. The Crown was held to have failed to establish its case on a second charge, that I had attended and spoken at an illegal gathering on the same tribal trust land.

On 11 June 1964 I was accused of uttering subversive statements. These referred to two speeches I had made at two separate ZANU rallies in which I claimed that because the laws of Rhodesia were unjust, 'many of our Courts are rubber stamps of injustice'. The two charges could have led to a ten-year prison sentence. But I was again acquitted, since the chief Crown witness admitted that the Courts were the administrative arm of the law and that in my speeches I had not been blaming the Courts.

But this was not the end of my legal battles arising out of my political activities. On 22 June 1964 I was arrested and formally remanded in custody by the Fort Victoria Magistrate's Court. The Attorney-General of Southern Rhodesia restrained any Court in Southern Rhodesia from granting me bail. I was kept in custody for two months before the Court hearing of my cases. I was alleged by the police to have instructed certain persons to do certain acts which contravened section 29(3)(b) of the Law and Order (Maintenance) Act, Chapter 39, which rendered liable to a seven-year prison sentence anyone found guilty of making statements which might defeat 'the purpose or intention of any law in force in Southern Rhodesia' or make public disorder likely.

Altogether there were forty-seven charges against me. The eleven main charges and thirty-three alternative charges arose out of my alleged contravention of the act mentioned above, and the other three main charges from a circular prepared by my Central Committee, which, as President of ZANU, I had signed.

The first eleven charges were heard from 24 to 28 August 1964. My National Chairman, Advocate Herbert Chitepo, then Director of Public Prosecutions, Tanzania, assisted by Advocate John Horn, conducted my defence in the Umtali Magistrate's Court. After four days of the Crown case, the Crown hopelessly failed to establish its case on any of the eleven main charges. My defence counsel had no case to meet, and so they applied for my discharge. The Crown did not even oppose the application! So I was acquitted on the eleven main charges and the thirty-three alternative charges also fell away. I was then left with three main charges arising out of a circular I had signed and circulated in the country. Now I had better explain the circular, and perhaps giving the exact text here would help the reader to see more clearly what was involved in the whole matter.

CALL TO ALL AFRICANS OF ZIMBABWE

The Central Committee of the Zimbabwe African National Union is now in possession of the full facts regarding the plans of the Rhodesian Front Government to declare unilateral independence.

The Farmers' Government is now conducting a trade alliance pact with Dr. Verwoerd's Republic of South Africa. Further the Government is also considering devaluing the pound (£1) in anticipation that Britain will not back it after their illegal step.

Parliament meets on the 28th July to consider the budget and then be sent home—probably for good under the present Constitution.

The Governor is being got rid of as soon as he goes on leave. It is strongly believed that Mr. Lilford—the godfather of the Rhodesian Front—will be named the new Governor who will sign papers sanctioning illegal independence.

New detention and concentration camps are now under construction along the Zambesi as additional to Gonakudzingwa and Wha Wha. The military training is taking place more vigorously than ever.

The Central Committee of ZANU now instructs all African people to do the following things:

1. Those who are working in towns, mines, farms, etc., should prepare to withdraw their monies from banks, building societies, and post office savings banks and put aside and buy large stocks of food which should be stored in a safe place.

2. Those in the reserves should not sell any more of their cattle, sheep, goats, pigs, and fowls. They should store large quantities of maize, ground-nuts, corn, etc.

3. Every family should study the surroundings of his home and locality for strategy.

4. Everyone should be ready to act as soon as the final instructions come from the President.

5. When the Government declares unilateral independence, all Africans must stop paying dipping fees, cattle fees, dog fees, and poll tax until an African Government is fully established in Zimbabwe.

6. Town residents must stop paying rents from the day unilateral independence is proclaimed.

7. Every man must have axes, bows and arrows, and other instruments ready to oppose physically unilateral independence and ACT as soon as unilateral independence is declared.

8. All African parents must withdraw their children from school as soon as illegal independence is declared.

The President of ZANU will declare a State of Emergency in the Party and country when time comes. That will be the time to act and do whatever you are ordered to do.

Zimbabwe is near—now you should lay down your lives, honour, and fortunes to make it a reality. LONG LIVE ZANU, LONG LIVE ZIMBABWE.

This historic document was drawn up by fifteen members of the Central Committee of the Zimbabwe African National Union.[1]

This circular was alleged first to contravene section 29(1) of the Law and Order (Maintenance) Act, Chapter 39, which rendered liable to a prison sentence of up to fourteen years anybody indicating or implying the desirability of an act likely to cause the physical injury or death of any person.

The second charge was that the circular had contravened section 29(3)(b), and the third the alleged contravention of section 44(2)(a) as read with 44(1)(a)(vii) of the Law and Order (Maintenance) Act, Chapter 39. This defined 'subversive statement' as one capable of inciting people to resist, other than by 'lawful means', officials in the 'maintenance of public order or safety or the application of law'. Anyone found guilty of a subversive statement was liable to a five-year prison sentence.

The words to which the law took exception were those in paragraph five of the circular (p. 42).

My defence counsel had previously applied for my discharge on these remaining three charges. When the Court reassembled on 4 September 1964 the magistrate, Mr. J. O. M. Jackson, gave his verdict on the three remaining counts. He said that a unilateral declaration of independence 'would be an unlawful act regarded in the light of the present Constitution' and that therefore anyone saying that taxes should not be paid to an unconstitutional government was not defeating the purpose of any law in force in Southern Rhodesia. The effect of such words was therefore irrelevant and I was acquitted of two of the charges.

The third had arisen from paragraph seven of the circular. I was asked whether, if a rebel government were set up in Rhodesia, I would ask people to oppose it 'violently by arms' and I said I would have no hesitation in so doing. I simply answered, 'I believe there's such a thing as a holy war.' I was found guilty and sentenced to twelve months' imprisonment because the magistrate said I was 'persuading people to arm themselves against a contingency which may never occur'.

[1] Rev. Ndabaningi Sithole, Robert Mugabe, Edson Zvobgo, Simon Muzenda, Advocates Simpson Mutambanengwe and Edson Sithole, Noel Mukano, Stanlake Samkange, Enos Nkala, Mrs. Maria Chakonda, Henry Hamadziripi, Nathan Shamuyarira, Morris Nyagumbo, Dr. Elisha Mutasa, and Francis Ngazimbi Musemburi. Advocate Herbert Chitepo and Morton Malianga were out of the country, and Leopold Takawira and Michael Mawema were in prison.

We lodged an appeal and on 15 January 1965 the Chief Justice, Sir Hugh Beadle, allowed the appeal, reasoning that the onus was on the Crown to show that a unilateral declaration of independence was likely to occur. 'The Crown has not', he said, 'shown that the appellant's statement means that it is desirable to do any act or acts which are likely to create public disorder.'

Both the Acting Judge President and the Appellate Judge Assistant agreed, so there was a unanimous judgement. The police had lost all forty-seven charges against me, but it cost me £960 for the entire defence, and friends pitched in to bear most of these expenses.

But the struggle for the liberation of Zimbabwe goes on. Imprisonment, detention, and restriction have become symbols of popular respect and esteem, and like all symbols, they do not end in themselves. They point beyond themselves. But they do not point into a vacuum. They point to the long, difficult road at the head of which lies the new Zimbabwe where man will count as man regardless of colour, creed, culture, and nationality.

PART TWO

Factors of Nationalism

CHAPTER 5

After World War II

The average white man in Africa is scared almost out of his senses by the rapid achievements of African nationalism. From the 1950s to the 1960s new African nations have come into being with almost a lightning speed, and those parts of Africa still held by the white man have not escaped the full impact of the existence of these new African states. The question has been asked: What is it that brought about, in the first place, this independence—bringing nationalistic feeling among a people who were otherwise docile and easily manageable by the white man? In the second place, what methods did African nationalism employ in the achievement of its goals?

It would be idle to single out one reason for this vigorous and colonialism-liquidating nationalism which swept the length and breadth of the vast continent of Africa (now the home of over 260,000,000 spread over Africa's 13,000,000 square miles of land). Like all movements, African nationalism has its roots in history, and without this historical foundation, the seemingly sudden African nationalism becomes inexplicable. There are chain causes which may be traced back to pre-European days of Africa. In our examination of the factors that gave rise to this African political phenomenon, it is well to bear in mind that all movements of consequence are preceded by ideas.

World War II, as many people have frequently noted, had a great deal to do with the awakening of the peoples of Africa. During the war the African came into contact with practically all the peoples of the earth. He met them on a life-and-death-struggle basis. He saw the so-called civilized and peaceful and orderly white people mercilessly butchering one another just as his so-called savage ancestors had done in tribal wars. He saw no difference between so-called primitive and so-called civilized man. In short, he saw through European pretensions that Africans were savages. This discovery, for indeed it was an eye-opening discovery, had a revolutionizing psychological impact on the African.

But more than this, World War II taught the African most powerful ideas. During the war the Allied Powers taught their subject peoples (and millions of them!) that it was not right for Germany to dominate other nations. They taught the subject peoples to fight and die for freedom, rather than live and be subjugated by Hitler. The subject peoples learnt the lesson well and responded magnificently, and they fought, and endured great hardship, and died, under the magic spell of freedom.

During the war the British officers appealed to the Africans to join the armed services, and so they began extensive propaganda against the Nazis. The British were not the only ones who did this; practically all the Allied Powers did the same thing. The following story typifies well the attitude of the African and other subject peoples.

'Away with Hitler! Down with him!' said the British officer.

'What's wrong with Hitler?' asked the unsuspecting African.

'He wants to rule the whole world,' snorted the British officer.

'What's wrong with that?'

'He's German, you see,' said the British officer, trying to appeal subtly to the African's tribal consciousness.

'What's wrong with his being German?'

'You see,' began the British officer, trying to explain in terms that would be conceivable to the African mind, 'it is not good for one tribe to rule another. Each tribe must rule itself. That's only fair. A German must rule Germans, an Italian, Italians, and a Frenchman, French people.'

But the extremely wary British officer did not say, 'A Briton, Britons'. What he said, however, carried weight with the Africans who rallied in thousands under the British flag. They joined the war to end the threat of Nazi domination.

After World War II, the Africans began to direct their British-aroused anti-domination spirit against the Allied Powers who had extensive colonial empires in Africa. (And the Asiatics did the same thing against colonial powers.) Various moves were made by Africans to end British and French dominance in Africa. 'You said it was wrong for the Germans to rule the world. It is also wrong for the British to dominate Africans.' It is also wrong for the French to dominate Africans.' It is also wrong for the Portuguese to dominate Africans. Thus African freedom-seekers and independence-hunters began to articulate their inmost longings and yearnings.

The big lesson that the African learned during the last war was that he fought and suffered to preserve the freedom he did not have back home. The lesson was driven home to him that the freedom for which so many Africans had died abroad was only enjoyed by the white man who ruled him. What was the difference between Hitler and the white man who denied him freedom on his own native land? Why should the African be used as an instrument for the freedom of the white man? Why must the African be used in his own country as a means to the ends of the white man? When was he also going to be free in the land of his birth? What should he do in order to become free in his own country? These questions crossed the minds of the Africans as they dreamed of the return of their country to its rightful owners.

Perhaps it will clarify our discussion if we trace briefly the African nationalist movement for full independence after the last world war. This nationalist movement was not confined only to Africa; and to understand the African situation better, it will reward us to put Africa aside for a moment and visit the gigantic continent of Asia and the Pacific islands.

Asian nationalism is most relevant to the question of African nationalism. Its roots cannot be sought in the post-World War II conditions but rather in the post-World War I conditions. It was only after World War I that Indian nationalism under the banner of the Indian National Congress, under the leadership of Mahatma Gandhi, grew in effective strength, formulated clear national objectives, and prosecuted vigorously the independence effort rooted in the mass, captained by India's intellectuals. In India the goods that were demanded persistently after World War I were only delivered after World War II. It is noteworthy that during the hostilities of 1939–1945 the Indians made a big contribution to the war. To the defeat of the Japanese in Burma, for instance, the Indians contributed 700,000 soldiers. They also played an important part in the conquest of Italian East Africa. By 1945 India had contributed 2,000,000 soldiers on a voluntary basis, and their distinguished war effort only strengthened their claims for independence. They had fought side by side with their 'soldier' masters, and never before had the fires of freedom burned in their hearts so fiercely and generated so much heat that threatened to burn up colonialism and imperialism root, trunk, and branch.

Burmese, Ceylonese, Indonesian, and French Indo-Chinese (i.e. Laotian, Cambodian, and Vietnamese) nationalism developed rapidly and dramatically at the end of World War I. It would appear that before this period the colonial powers had succeeded in suppressing the political expression of these people, but this only served to concentrate their political feelings with such intensity that when

LIBRARY — LUTHERAN SCHOOL
OF THEOLOGY AT CHICAGO

these feelings finally broke through the strong walls of colonialism and imperialism, it became next to impossible to control them. In spite of the tireless efforts on the part of the colonial powers to placate these ardent nationalists between World War I and World War II, in the post-World War II era the colonial powers capitulated with the grace of a reluctant regent who hands over the throne to its rightful owner, and with the pride of a schoolmaster who has to give way to one of his brilliant pupils, 'You should do well after all the years I taught you.'

What was the meaning of independence to these people ? It meant that millions of people, who had hitherto lived, moved, and had their being under foreign domination, who had ceased to be regarded as persons but only as means to foreign ends, were now persons who counted for something in the land of their birth. That sense of belonging to their country had been lost since the advent of foreign rule, and man is less than man unless he belongs to something in which he has a say and over which he has a certain measure of control. Secondly, independence meant that the million square miles of land which belonged to these people, but were used primarily for the interests of the foreign ruler, could now be used first and foremost for the interests of the natives themselves. It meant that what the soil now produced, what the natural forests put out, what mineral wealth the soil held below it, and what the rivers yielded in the way of food materials could now be disposed of at the will, and for the benefit, of the natives themselves. In short, both human and natural resources were now to be used for the sole benefit of the natives themselves instead of foreigners. These countries ceased to play to the tune of foreigners. They now played to their own tune, and nothing is healthier and better for the human personality.

It is noteworthy here that after the war millions of people who were liberated from the colonial clutches, became a shining example to the non-independent peoples of what independence actually meant. The non-independent peoples felt very deeply about their own independence-denying status, and they felt that something had to be done to terminate their unsatisfactory status. So it was that the independence-laden Asian atmosphere began to flow towards Africa and it only served to quicken the independence spirit which was already swaying many a heart in Africa.

From what we have said so far, it would appear that the period between the end of World War I (1918) and the end of World War II (1945) was a period of incubation of Asian and Near East nationalism, and the period after World War II its hatching period and one of consolidating its achievements.

It is to be noted that after millions of people had been liberated in Asia and the Near East this unprecedented event in the history of mankind could not fail to have an appreciable impact on the continent of Africa, most of whose inhabitants were still moving in the shackles and fetters of European colonialism and imperialism. The peoples of Africa saw that the peoples of Asia and the Near East had liberated themselves by hook or by crook. As the independence-laden Asian atmosphere reached Africa it only served to strengthen the African 'freedom spirit' which was already getting impatient and was now desperately seeking to crush the crust of colonialism and imperialism which had been encasing it for decades.

On the continent of Africa, after long, uninterrupted, and undisputed colonial rule by European powers, the real rumblings and murmurings and eventually the onslaughts of African nationalism did not begin until during and after World War II. The existence of a free and independent Ethiopia and Liberia since 1040 B.C. and A.D. 1847, respectively, and also that of an independent Egypt since 1922, served as fuel to the burning freedom fires within the breasts of millions of non-independent Africans. When Libya and Ghana became independent in 1951 and 1957 respectively, this fired the imagination of the African people enormously, and a chain-reaction for independence began with more vigour than ever before. The liberation of Africa from European domination had begun. It was no longer 'Down with Hitler!'; it was now, 'Down with British colonialism and imperialism!' The people became more determined to see that British domination went the way threatened Nazi domination went.

Perhaps quoting from some of the outstanding African political leaders will serve to make clear what I am trying to say. President Nasser said:

We cannot, under any circumstances, remain aloof from the terrible and sanguinary struggle going on in Africa today between five million whites and 200 million Africans. . . . The peoples of Africa will continue to look at us, who guard the northern gate and constitute their link with all the outside world. We will never . . . be able to relinquish our responsibility to support, with all our might, the spread of enlightenment and civilization to the remotest depth of the jungle. . . .

The dark continent is now the scene of a strange and excited turbulence. . . . We shall not, in any circumstances, stand idly by in the face of what is going on in Africa in the belief that it will not affect or concern us. . . .

I will continue to dream of the day when I will find in Cairo a great African Institute dedicated . . . to an enlightened African consciousness, and to sharing with others from all over the world in the work of advancing the peoples of the continent.[1]

Later events proved that these were not empty words. At the time when the Kenyan African nationalists were finding it too hot to remain in Kenya without being sent to the gallows or long-term imprisonment by the British colonial administration there, President Nasser housed them and gave them the necessary facilities to carry on their nationalist struggle from Cairo. At one time Cairo became the harbour of African nationalists, who were allowed to open their offices there, and such nationalist organizations as the Kenya African National Union, the Congress of Uganda, the African National Congress of South Africa, the Pan-Africanist Congress, the Zimbabwe African National Union, the People's Caretaker Council, the Mozambique Liberation Front, the Basutoland African National Congress, and the South-West African nationalist organizations, carried on their work from Cairo.

Dr. Kwame Nkrumah, Prime Minister of the then Gold Coast, said:

Freedom of the Gold Coast will be a fountain of inspiration from which other African colonial territories can draw when the time comes for them to strike for their freedom. An independent Gold Coast will encourage the remaining dependent territories of Africa to continue their struggle for freedom and independence. . . . To me, independence for the Gold Coast is meaningless unless it is linked up with the total liberation of the continent of Africa.[2]

Even on the day that the Gold Coast gained her full independence from Britain, though remaining within the British Commonwealth of Nations, Prime Minister Kwame Nkrumah still reminded the sixty-six nations represented at the Ghana Freedom celebrations that Ghana 'would assist all African peoples in their pursuit of freedom and social progress'.[3]

Like President Nasser, Dr. Kwame Nkrumah housed many African nationalists from all over Africa and he remained true to his

[1] Gamal Abdul-Nasser, *Egypt's Liberation: The Philosophy of the Revolution*, Public Affairs Press, Washington, 1955, pp. 109–11.

[2] *Phylon*, Fourth Quarter, 1955, p. 407.

[3] *The Christian Science Monitor*, 6 March 1957.

expressed sentiments of the liberation of Africa. His Pan-Africanist magazine *The Voice of Africa*, with a picture of a giant African breaking asunder the chains of many decades and a picture of a red flame on the cover, gripped the imagination of many Africans. The chain-breaking African giant symbolized the independence-winning African, and the red flame the burning fires of freedom in the hearts of the African millions.

The hatred against Hitler was transferred to European colonialism now that Nazi domination had been done away with. An Asiatic once said to me, 'We owe our independence to Adolf Hitler!'

Here then is the paradox of history, that the Allied Powers, by effectively liquidating the threat of Nazi world domination, set in motion those powerful forces which are now liquidating, with equal effectiveness, European domination in Africa. As one Moroccan put it, 'Our struggle against France is a carry-over from Hitler.' The emergence and the march of African nationalism were in reality a boomerang on the colonial powers. They fired the anti-domination bullet at Nazi Germany, but the same bullet was also, in turn, successfully fired at them!

To start with, the outside world, especially the Western world, the perpetrators of colonialism and imperialism which denied the African full citizenship in the land of his birth, thought that African nationalism was anti-white through and through, and were therefore not sympathetic to it. Many African nationalists were branded as rebels and subjected to the severest penalties for their nationalist activities. In India, for instance, Mahatma Gandhi, the perfecter of the passive-resistance weapon, became a regular jailbird for his nationalist activities, which finally brought about full independence for more than 360,000,000 people. Nationalist Prime Minister Nehru was another illustrious Indian jailbird. In Morocco, nationalist Sultan Mohammed V was deposed by France in 1953, and exiled to Madagascar, but the nationalist struggle kept on until France was obliged to grant Morocco full independence. The future President Kwame Nkrumah of Ghana was imprisoned for his nationalist activities which were construed by the then British administration to be seditious. The future President Hastings Banda of Malawi spent thirteen months in the Gwelo prison, Rhodesia, on the ground that the African National Congress of the then Nyasaland, of which he was president, had hatched a plot to massacre white people in Central Africa. President Jomo Kenyatta has served a seven-year prison sentence for allegedly master-minding the Mau Mau revolt.

Dr. Kenneth Kaunda served a nine-month jail sentence for allegedly inciting people to violence. The writer himself served a twelve-month jail sentence for an allegedly subversive statement calling upon the African people to boycott the 1962 Rhodesian elections. What all this adds up to is that Westerners hated the African nationalists so much that an African nationalist was usually regarded as the hater of the white man. African nationalism became, in many cases, identified with communism to which the capitalist West was opposed.

This view, though widely prevalent, was nevertheless wrong. African nationalism was directed against European domination, just as the attention of the Allied Powers was directed against Nazism and all that it stood for, not against the German people as such. When, for instance, Canada, Australia, and New Zealand set about demanding full independence from Britain, that was not an anti-British move. What these countries wanted was the removal of the domination of the United Kingdom Government and no more. What the African wanted was not to drive the white man out of Africa, but rather to have his full independence. Later events in now independent African countries have proved European fears to be baseless. As a matter of fact these independent African countries have now more white people than they had before independence, and these white people stay in these countries of their own accord. Many more come to live in these countries of their own choice. Nowhere in any part of independent Africa have the white people as a race been victims of African nationalism except before independence. Many white people, for instance in Kenya and Zambia, have made personal testimonies that their fears of the imagined African nationalist hatred of the white man had been entirely unjustified.

Perhaps we should now examine how it came about that most whites conceived the plausible but erroneous idea that, in general, African nationalism was aimed at the white people. The average white man in Africa equated his existence with white domination. He felt that the white man could not possibly live in Africa as an ordinary citizen like everyone else. He could only live as a ruler. No European rule, no European existence. The white man could not think otherwise. The laws of the country which he made took every care to see that every white man was insulated against African competition. A dual system of jobs and salaries and wages was ingeniously contrived. Jobs were divided into European and African, and European jobs often carried high salaries and wages. Everywhere in European-ruled Africa, the African gave way to the European because the European was the ruler. The white man lived off the fat of the land. Economically he held the fat end of the wedge whereas the African held the thin end. Anyone therefore who set himself against European domination logically set himself against the white man. To try to choke white domination was like trying to choke the white man himself; hence white opposition to African nationalism.

But at the back of the mind of the white man, or deep down in his heart, somewhere in his subconscious, there was the constant fear that if the African took over he would treat the European as the European had treated him. The European feared his own bad treatment of the African if this was reversed. Hence, his labelling African nationalism as anti-European was at best a rational defence mechanism around his own selfish interests summed up in the phrase 'white supremacy' with which we shall deal later on in this book.

But, of course, there was all the difference between the white man and white domination, although the white man was so used to riding on the shoulders of Africans that he could not be persuaded to believe that he could still live and move and have his being in Africa after the Africans had thrown him off their shoulders. In Africa there is still enough room for many more people who desire to live on an equal footing. The 'domination space', however, has shrunk never to spring back again.

Talking to a 'University of Life Forum' in Newburyport, Massachusetts in November 1956, I tried to show that 'Africa needs the friendship of the West, and the West the friendship of Africa. But while this is perfectly true, it is also equally true that Africa does not need, and does not want, the domination of the West, just as the West would not want to be dominated by Africa.'

To illustrate further that African nationalism opposed, not the white man, but white domination, I quote once more from Kwame Nkrumah, then Prime Minister of Ghana: 'I stand for no racialism, no discrimination against any race or individual, but I am unalterably opposed to imperialism in any form.'

'What we stand against,' said a Rhodesian African politician, 'is not the white man, but this obnoxious practice of subordinating the African to European interests so that they [Africans] become things to be manipulated by the white man according to the whims of his temper. We want to be accepted as men by men of other races.'

In South Africa where the Nationalist Party in power is determined to retain white domination over non-whites, a new spirit among both black and white is pressing for a new independence for the downtrodden peoples of that land. In July 1955 the Congress of the People composed of some 3,000 people was convened and a Freedom Charter was adopted. The Charter ran:

We, the people of South Africa, declare for all our country and the world to know: that South Africa belongs to all who live in it, black and white, and that no government can justly claim authority unless it is based on the will of the people; that our people have been robbed of their birthright to land, liberty, and peace by a form of government founded on injustice and inequality; that our country will never be prosperous or free until all our people live in brotherhood, enjoying equal rights and opportunities; that only a democratic state, based on the will of all the people, can secure to all their birthright without distinction of colour, race, sex, or belief; and therefore, we the people of South Africa, black and white together—equals, countrymen, and brothers—adopt this Freedom Charter. And we pledge ourselves together, sparing nothing of our strength and courage, until the democratic changes here set out have been won.[1]

The Reverend George Gray, an American Negro with a very keen insight into the course of human history, once said to me, as we discussed, on the campus of the Andover-Newton Theological Seminary, the important results of World War II:

'The last world war did not teach the subject peoples the spirit of independence. This was already there. People had long felt the poignant injustice of subordination and discrimination. They had no means hitherto of vocalizing and dramatizing their deep-seated grievances. World War II focused these grievances more intensely and gave them an effective expression. World War II did not give birth to the spirit of independence, but rather gave expression to the spirit which was already there. Pre-World War II conditions broke down the high walls of European domination. . . . World War II was a very powerful instrument in forestalling Nazi world domination, and it has been equally effective in ringing the death-bell of European colonialism.'

T. Walter Wallbank said:

The two decades separating World War I from World War II were formative years of African nationalism. On the surface, little was to be seen, but pressures and aspirations were building up that broke loose with astonishing force following the end of hostilities in 1946. . . .

[1] As Quoted in 'Treason in South Africa', an article by George M. Houser in *The Christian Century*, 6 March 1957, p. 289.

If the seeds of African nationalism were sown in the two decades between wars, they matured with astonishing speed after 1939. A number of factors explain this growth. To justify their cause the Allied nations, such as Britain, France, and the United States, promised to speed up the tempo of self-government for colonial powers.[1]

Before we end this chapter we may as well define and explain what we mean by the concept 'African nationalism'. It should be noted that the concept as used here is restricted to the African context. It is not a general but specific concept, only applicable to the African situation. It has no universal application except within this specified context. We may define African nationalism as a feeling. Unless it is a feeling, then it cannot be identified. But it is not a general feeling, like the feeling we have for water or our friends or enemies. It is a special feeling of a political nature. Unless that African feeling is of a political nature it cannot qualify as African nationalism. We may now extend our definition thus: African nationalism is a political feeling manifesting itself against European rule in favour of African rule. It is only in this context of the African desire to rule himself as against the European practice of ruling the African that African nationalism can be a conceivable political phenomenon.

Since the coming of the European to Africa European rule had been the order of the day. The European did not rule Africa according to the precedents and demands of democracy back in his own country. His government was not, to borrow the language of another, of the people by the people for the people, but rather, government of the Europeans by the Europeans for the Europeans. May it be remembered here that no people or nation rules for the benefit of another. Similarly, Europeans could not rule for the benefit of the peoples of Africa, but for their own benefit. Their government is therefore better characterized not by the term *democracy*, which would be a gross misnomer, but by the term of my own coinage *eurocracy*—i.e. rule of Europeans, by Europeans, for Europeans. It is important to note that the whole continent of Africa, since the Berlin Conference of 1884–5, was confronted by this disturbing factor of *eurocracy*—European rule, which posed the question of African rule, which we may call here *afrocracy*. African nationalism may therefore be defined as a political feeling seeking relentlessly to eliminate

[1] T. W. Wallbank, *Contemporary Africa: Continent in Transition*, Anvil Series, D. van Nostrand Co. Ltd., Princeton and London, revised edition 1964, pp. 51 and 59.

eurocracy by supplanting it with *afrocracy*. It should be further noted that *eurocracy* was the target of African nationalism which it sought to exterminate root, stem, and branch, and that African nationalism tended to die with the death of *eurocracy* but left *afrocracy* in the saddle. African nationalism was merely an effective instrument of establishing African rule.

CHAPTER 6

The U.N. Factor

A survey of those factors which helped African nationalism to grow and to achieve its goal would be incomplete if the role of the United Nations Organization was left out. But it should be borne in mind that, like World War II, the United Nations did not give birth to African nationalism, but rather it provided it with a powerful forum and an inestimable international moral authority which, though lacking the necessary teeth to bite deep into, and tear up, colonialism at the more accelerated rate the African nationalists would have desired, was a powerful instrument in the long and dangerous process of dismantling colonialism. In this chapter we would therefore like to examine in broad outline the interaction between African nationalism and the United Nations, an organization which served to quicken the pace of liberating the continent of Africa.

There does not appear to be any relation between it and the League of Nations which came into being after World War I. The only African countries that were members of the League were Ethiopia, Liberia, and Egypt, and at that time these independent African countries did not think and act in terms of the African continent as such. When they occasionally did try to verbalize something for the benefit of the African people in general, what did their voice amount to compared with more than 60 other members? They were less than 5 per cent. of the total membership. Moreover, the League of Nations as such, in theory and in practice, did not concern itself with colonialism in general, beyond the mandated territories. It was principally concerned with the burning question of collective security. The United States of America never became a member of this international body. It clung to the Monroe doctrine of non-intervention in the affairs of Europe, and generally the League of Nations was regarded as a European affair in spite of the multiracial and multi-national composition of its membership.

The United Nations Organization came into being in August, 1945. Some of the articles of the Charter will throw more light on the relevance of the United Nations to African nationalism. Article 73 runs:

Members of the United Nations which have or assume responsibilities for the administration of territories whose peoples have not yet attained a full measure of self-government recognise the principle that the interests of the inhabitants of these territories are paramount, and accept as a sacred trust the obligation to promote to the utmost, within the system of international peace and security established by the present Charter, the well-being of the inhabitants of these territories, and, to this end: . . .

(b) to develop self-government, to take due account of the political aspirations of the peoples, and to assist them in the progressive development of their free political institutions, according to the particular circumstances of each territory and its peoples and their varying stages of development. . . .

This was an important declaration with regard to non-self-governing territories. Article 75 refers to the international trusteeship system and Article 76 of the Charter, which spells out Article 75 a little more fully, runs:

The basic objectives of the trusteeship system, in accordance with the purposes of the United Nations laid down in Article 1 of the present Charter shall be: . . .

(b) to promote the political, economic, social, and educational advancement of the inhabitants of the trust territories, and their progressive development towards self-government or independence as may be appropriate to the particular circumstances of each territory and its peoples and the freely expressed wishes of the peoples concerned, and as may be provided by the terms of each trusteeship agreement.

Both Articles 73 and 76(b) make direct reference to the desirability of self-government or independence of non-self-governing and trust territories, and these declarations coincided with the aspirations and goals of African nationalism. The United Nations in setting down these declarations marked the trend the liberation of non-independent countries was to follow. Clark M. Eichelberger summed up the situation:

Indeed, as the second decade of the United Nations ends, only a few scattered peoples are without self-government. Less than 2 per cent. of the world's population now lives under colonial rule.

The rapidity of this development was not anticipated at San Francisco, although its seeds were planted in the organization. The Charter of the United Nations has become a charter of liberty under which the colonial peoples aspire for freedom. The organization itself, particularly the General Assembly and the Trusteeship Council, has provided the forums in which appeals for freedom can be made. Now, one-third of the membership of the United Nations is made up of new states. They have made a profound change in the power balance of the organization.[1]

The colonial powers seem to have been resigned to the inevitability of self-government for their colonial peoples, but what they openly opposed was not so much African nationalism but the speed at which it should be achieved. They felt it was too revolutionary. They wanted it to follow an evolutionary pattern. In other words, they wanted it to move at the rate they themselves wanted to set. But since African nationalism was a political feeling which was not generated in them but in the African it could not move at their pace but at the pace of the African. Youth can only move at the pace of youth, and not at the pace of old age. This was the situation in Africa when the colonial peoples revolted against colonialism.

To come back to the beginning of the United Nations. In August 1945 the major colonial powers were Britain, France, Belgium, Holland, and the U.S.A. The membership of the United Nations stood at 50 in 1945 and by 1960 it had risen to 104. The close of 1965 saw the membership of the United Nations standing at 115. The last remaining non-independent countries are swelling this figure as they become fully independent.

A close study of the voting trends at the United Nations shows an interesting fact. There are distinct group arrangements for consultation and general support, and these are based on common interests. According to voting patterns which have emerged in the course of the life of the United Nations, one can line up these: the Western bloc, the Soviet bloc, the South American bloc, and the Afro-Asian-Arab bloc. (The Commonwealth group cannot possibly be regarded as a voting bloc. In theory and in practice it has not pretended to approach problems raised at the United Nations as a group. The existence of the Western voting group in which many members belong to the Commonwealth, and the existence of the African members who are in the Commonwealth or in the French Community, and who are also active members of the Afro-Asian-Arab bloc, have dealt the possibility of the Commonwealth voting bloc a death-blow.) The Afro-Asian-Arab bloc is the largest voting bloc at the United Nations, and questions affecting African independence have received its full support. The Western bloc has tended to

[1] Clark M. Eichelberger, *The United Nations: The First 20 Years*, Harper and Row, London, 1965, p. 14.

accede to the independence demands of the African delegates, but has often differed on the question of timing and method. The South American bloc has also tended to support the various moves for African independence. When everything has been added up all voting blocs at the United Nations accept the fundamental principle of African freedom and independence.

If we look at the membership of the United Nations from another angle, we find that at the beginning, in 1945, it consisted of colonial powers, of those who had no colonies, and of those who had lost their colonies. After 1945 those who had been given their freedom and independence were rapidly admitted into the membership of the United Nations. In other words, those who were still fresh with the wounds of colonialism soon found themselves face to face with those who had inflicted those wounds. Colonialists and anti-colonialists found themselves members of the same organization enjoying equal status. It does not require any stretch of imagination to see that the anti-colonialists vowed to give any aid to any programme that was designed to exterminate colonialism, under which they themselves had suffered untold indignities and humiliations, and from which they had just victoriously emerged. African nationalism utilized to great advantage these anti-colonialist attitudes and sentiments. No anti-colonialist oration was considered great among the Afro-Asian-Arab bloc unless it vividly castigated, vehemently denounced, and uncompromisingly rejected colonialism.

Perhaps the steps the United Nations took to see that the non-independent countries of Africa became independent should now be considered. In accordance with the United Nations Charter, Article 75, seven African countries were created Trust Territories and placed under the supervision of the United Nations, and these were Tanganyika, British Cameroons, British Somaliland, British Togoland, French Cameroons, French Togoland, Ruanda-Urundi, and Somaliland.

The supervision of Trust Territories was placed in the hands of the Trusteeship Council, on which all colonial powers were represented. Annual reports were received from administering powers, and debated at some length. As some of these were unsatisfactory to countries like India, the Council devised new procedures, such as sending U.N. Missions to the Trust Territories themselves, or hearing petitioners in New York. Abdullahi Issa of Somalia, Sylvanus Olympio of Togo, Julius Nyerere of Tanganyika (now Tanzania), to mention a few, appeared before the Council as petitioners and made a deep impression on delegates. They wrote and circulated memoranda which criticized the administrative practices of the administering powers, and called on the United Nations to insist on the implementation of the principles of its own Charter, particularly self-determination and the enjoyment of full human rights. The critical eye kept on the Trust Territories by the Council was the strongest single factor that led to the decolonization of Tanganyika (1960), British Cameroons (1960), British Togoland (1960), French Cameroons (1960), French Togoland (1960), Somalia (1960), and Ruanda-Urundi (now Rwanda and Burundi) (1962). This represented tremendous gains for African nationalism. Perhaps we can now turn to other territories outside the scope of the Trusteeship Council. What part did the United Nations play in the liberation of these territories?

It would require a separate volume to assess the full impact of the United Nations on the continent of Africa. Only a few salient facts can be discussed here. The existence of the United Nations had an important psychological role in the emancipation of Africa. It set the tone and the international standard in its very Charter when it called for the self-determination of all people. Just imagine the impact on millions of people who had been taught and told for many decades that they were not fit to rule themselves; that they had been created to be ruled by the white race only; that their place under the sun was second- or third-class citizenship in the land of their birth; that they were only equals among themselves but not with any people outside their own; and that their chief function was to draw water and hew wood for foreigners who ruled them. And then an international organization reverses this whole trend by telling them they were equals of everyone else, and were entitled to self-government, freedom, and independence, and to first-class citizenship; and that they existed to further their own ends not those of others. Only those who have gone through the actual experience of being treated like things in the land of their birth, can appreciate the emotional and psychological impact of such pronouncements from a platform as lofty as that of the United Nations.

To the French *colons* the United Nations was a threatening symbol that pointed to the destruction of French colonialism, on which they had flourished and grown fat; to the British settlers and colonists the United Nations was an evil omen which promised to liquidate the 'European way of life'—Europeans high, Africans low—and to disrupt altogether their avowed doctrine of white supremacy;

but to the non-independent African, the United Nations was a symbol that moved him to the very core of his independence-seeking being. Like any symbol, the United Nations did not end in itself. It did not point to itself. It pointed beyond itself, but not to the vacant beyond. It pointed to the sequestration of independence-denying colonialism and to the eagerly awaited realization of African sovereign independence.

The debate on colonial questions began in the Committee of Information at the insistence of India, reaching its climax in the historic session of the General Assembly in September–October, 1960, soon after the admission of the largest number of African states in history—eleven of them. World leaders of the day all spoke in that debate, Nikita Khrushchev staying in New York most of the session to lead the Russian delegation. By mid-December a general agreement had been reached on what became known as a declaration on the granting of independence to colonial countries and people.[1] The effect of the declaration was to strip colonialism of all its legitimacy; others would say it outlawed colonialism. Colonial powers were instructed by the declaration and subsequent resolution to grant independence to colonial people without delay. Lack of education or material insufficiency was not to be used to delay independence. Support was pledged for those struggling to achieve this objective. Eighty-nine states voted for the declaration, none against, but the following nine abstained—Britain, United States, France, Portugal, Spain, Belgium, South Africa, Dominican Republic, and Australia. The common element among most of those states is not far to seek. The fact that South Africa and Portugal did not vote against the resolution is an indication of the measure of success achieved by the United Nations in mobilizing opinion against colonialism.

When the Committee of Twenty-Four was established early in 1962, African leaders in Central Africa, notably Dr. Kenneth Kaunda of Zambia, Joshua Nkomo and myself from Southern Rhodesia, and Europeans like the Rev. Michael Scott and the Hon. R. S. G. Todd, had our first opportunity to bring the problems of our region to the attention of the world body. We petitioned every year until

[1] General Assembly Resolution 1514 (XV). In pursuance of this resolution the Assembly established the Committee of 17 (now 24), whose full title is: 'The Special Committee on the Situation regarding the Implementation of the Declaration on the Granting of Independence to Colonial Countries and Peoples'.

1966, wrote memoranda, and lobbied delegations of all countries. In 1966, the Committee adopted the procedure of holding its meetings in Africa in order to exert more pressure on administering powers, and also to let some delegates see the conditions in parts of Africa at first-hand. Our representatives have continued to appear before the Committee at its meetings in Africa.

The influence of the U.N. on Africa in particular, and developing countries in general, is not limited to political questions. The Specialized Agencies have done sterling work in the transfer of capital and skills from developed and developing countries in order to bridge the North–South gap. I have emphasized throughout this book the need to develop Africa's human and natural resources for the sole benefit of its own people. To do this effectively Africa needs skilled manpower. The Specialized Agencies have put their shoulder to this wheel. A study of the various statistical tables appearing in Vernon McKay's *Africa in World Politics* throws some interesting light on the activities of the United Nations in Africa. In the period 1950–51 the programme for technical assistance to Africa cost the United Nations $442,000, whereas in 1961–2 the cost for this period was $20,088,000. This is fifty times as much as the 1950–51 cost. Between 1950 and 1960 forty-five African countries were supplied with 2,937 U.N. experts and 2,098 U.N. fellowships for research and study. In 1962 the World Bank loaned 16 African countries $929,000,000. This represented about 15 per cent. of all the loans by the Bank.[1] One has only to go through the activities of the various secondary organs of the United Nations to see the influence the United Nations is exerting on Africa.

This, however, should not be taken to mean that the United Nations had no serious shortcomings in general; we are here merely considering its influence on African nationalism, which it greatly stimulated. After World War II international opinion and sentiment had crystallized against colonialism and imperialism, and this trend happily coincided with the growing African nationalism. Part of what the United Nations wanted to see in this world—namely, national freedom and independence, full human rights, sound economic development, and a determined struggle against all inequality in its political, social, and economic forms—was also the goal of African nationalism. Both the United Nations and African nationalism used each other to realize some of their respec-

[1] Vernon A. McKay, *Africa in World Politics*, Harper and Row, London, 1963, pp. 56–7 and 65.

tive goals which happened to coincide. The relevant sections of the United Nations Charter could only be expressed through the feelings of the downtrodden inhabitants of the various African countries, and these feelings had been epitomized in African nationalism. The United Nations would not have made the present political impact on Africa unless its programme, in one way or another, coincided with the aims, objectives, aspirations, and demands of African nationalism. African nationalists fully accepted the United Nations for this reason. If, on the other hand, the United Nations had worked against the interests of African nationalism, it is inconceivable that they would have co-operated with it. They would have rejected it without a second thought.

However, the decolonization process suffered two serious setbacks in 1965. The International Court of Justice refused to pronounce decisive judgement on the two cases on the mandated status of South-West Africa. I will not examine the issues in those cases, but briefly Liberia and Ethiopia wanted the indigenous people of South-West Africa to rule themselves and not be ruled by a foreign government seated in Pretoria. Secondly, the 200,000 white settlers in Rhodesia declared their independence of Britain unilaterally, as we have discussed elsewhere. The South African and Rhodesian settlers were denounced in very strong language, and several excellent resolutions were passed, but there was no practical result for the Africans. Most Africans realized that although the United Nations can exert strong moral pressures, and create a psychological climate for change, it has no teeth to bite those who abstained from the 1960 declaration. In other words, it can only go as far as the latter want it to go. It was as well that most Africans had not seen the U.N. in its proper perspective; if they had, it might have reduced the momentum that African nationalism in fact gathered.

The fate of international organizations has been decided on African soil. The League of Nations failed to stop Italian aggression in Ethiopia in 1936. It never recovered its prestige and was to be ignored three years later when war broke out in Europe. The United Nations is now facing a severe test over South-West Africa, Rhodesia, South Africa, and the Portuguese Territories. The régimes of these countries negate every major principle on which the United Nations is founded. Economic sanctions, which failed dismally in Ethiopia in 1936, are being tried against Rhodesia. At the time of writing (1967) the Rhodesian economy had not been hurt by sanctions. It did not appear that they would bite or hurt in future.

CHAPTER 7

The Pan-African Factor

In an earlier chapter of this book I stated that events of consequence go back into history. They cannot be fully explained by their present circumstances. The same thing can be said of African nationalism. It cannot be explained only in terms of the post-World War II conditions, nor can it be explained only in terms of the conditions after World War I. Whatever theory we may advance as to the origin of African nationalism it must eventually go back to a set of historical circumstances that gave rise to a phenomenon of 'consciousness of kind' without which African nationalism or Pan-Africanism would have been next to impossible. It is inconceivable how Pan-Africanism, which sired African nationalism, could have so successfully appealed to the West Indians and the Negroes of America as well as to the peoples of Africa living under widely divergent political, economic, cultural, historical, and geographical circumstances unless their common denominator—their only one reconciling, fundamental basis—was this 'consciousness of kind'. This 'consciousness of kind' is not something that was born with these people involved in Pan-Africanism and African nationalism, but it grew in the course of their divergent histories. There were particular historical circumstances which fused to produce this fact of 'consciousness of kind'. Perhaps the following incident might illustrate the point better.

When I was in Naples in February 1955, on my way to the United States, I startled six of my white missionary friends when I suddenly ordered our taxi-driver to stop.

'What's the matter, Ndaba?' the Reverend John Marsh asked me.

'There's a friend of mine over there,' and no sooner had I said that than I banged the door of the taxi behind me and hurried across the street to see my friend who also had seen me. We just fell into each other's arms. I was so happy to see him. He was so happy to see me. The only word I could understand from him was 'Somalia', and when I reciprocated this with 'Rhodesia', he apparently understood me, and cried, 'Africa'. I repeated, 'Yes, Africa.' We shook hands again and indicated by gestures that we were well and that Africa was going up, up, up. We shook our heads that it was no longer going down, down, down. I bade him goodbye. I had to hurry back to our taxi which I had most unceremoniously stopped and which was impatiently waiting for my return.

'What was that, Ndaba?' the Reverend John Marsh asked.

'I don't know except that he's an African like me,' I said.

'But we thought he was a friend of yours!' the Reverend John Marsh cried with surprise.

'Oh, yes, he is, although I have never met him before.'

What had happened was this. For four weeks I had not seen a black face. I had been completely lost in a vast ocean of white faces. When suddenly a black face appeared in this vast ocean of white faces, 'consciousness of kind' seized me and gave me wings and I flew across the street, and there united with my own kind, and in spite of the language difficulty between us, my heart and his throbbed in unison. We communicated the warmth of our hearts to each other.

This is only a personal example of the 'consciousness of kind', but it does illustrate the point. One can sense a 'consciousness of kind' between Great Britain and the white members of the Commonwealth of Nations—Canada, Australia, and New Zealand. One can also sense it between the United States of America and Great Britain, and among the Western nations as a white group in contrast to other groups like the Asian and the African groups. But of course there are other factors which tend to modify one way or another this concept of 'consciousness of kind'. The concepts of 'consciousness of destination' and 'identity of interests' tend to keep in check the racial elements inherent in 'consciousness of kind'.

African nationalism's origin must be sought in these psychological dimensions we have here called 'consciousness of kind', and this requires an examination of that environment which gave rise to the movement of these dimensions. Among the Ndau-speaking people of Rhodesia there has grown up a saying which is much in circulation. It goes 'Muyungu ndiye ndiye' (The white man is the same the world over). By this they mean to say that the white man the world over likes to rule and humiliate the black man. This saying may sound exaggerated, but when it is viewed against the background of what happened in European-ruled Africa where the black man was often discriminated against, humiliated, denied full citizenship in his own country, and in the United States where the Negro was often discriminated against, relegated to non-citizen status, and sometimes lynched, the truth of this saying becomes evident. W. E. Burghardt DuBois had this to say:

After the Egyptian and Indian, the Greek and the Roman, the Teuton and Mongolian, the Negro is a sort of seventh son, born with a veil, and gifted with a second-sight in this American world—a world which yields him no true self-consciousness, but only lets him see himself through the revelation of the other world. It is a peculiar sensation, this double-consciousness, this sense of always looking at one's self through the eyes of others, of measuring one's soul by the tape of a world that looks on in amused contempt and pity. One ever feels his twoness—an American, or Negro; two souls, two thoughts, two unreconciled strivings; two warring ideals in one dark body, whose dogged strength alone keeps it from being torn asunder.

The history of the American Negro is the history of this strife—this longing to attain self-conscious manhood, to merge his double self into a better and truer self. In this merging he wishes neither of the older selves to be lost. He would not Africanize America, for America has too much to teach the world and Africa. He would not bleach his Negro soul in a flood of White Americanism, for he knows that Negro blood has a message for the world. He simply wishes to make it possible for a man to be both a Negro and an American without being cursed and spat upon by his fellows, without having the doors of opportunity closed roughly in his face.[1]

European rule in Africa had created two separate environments throughout the length and breadth of Africa. In South Africa, for example, apartheid—that is, racial apartness—has created a special environment for the African. In this environment the African is denied full citizenship in his own country. He is discriminated against on no other ground than that he was born black. In Rhodesia, and what was then Northern Rhodesia but is now Zambia, political, economic, and social inequality greeted the African everywhere. In short, in every European-ruled country a special environment in which the African was treated as though he did not exist—denied the right to vote, to hold a job according to ability, and to earn according to qualifications, experience, and merit—was created from the Cape to Cairo, and from Africa's Eastern Horn to her Western Bulge. Whether the white man who happened to rule an African country was British, French, Portuguese, Spanish, Belgian, or Afrikaner, his treatment of the black man was fundamentally the same. This practice of oppressing the African gave rise to the fact of 'consciousness of kind' which flowered in African nationalism.

Similarly, the same thing was experienced by the American

[1] W. E. B. DuBois, *The Souls of the Blacks*, Fawcett World Library, New York, pp. 16-17.

Negro. His own environment of being discriminated against and humiliated in his own country was the same as the one in which the African lived. In other words, wherever there was a black man the white man denied him those ordinary human rights, and the universal denial of these rights to the black man by the white man gave birth to the 'consciousness of kind' among the black peoples wherever they were, and hence the universal appeal of Pan-Africanism to the millions of Africans, West Indians, and Negroes in spite of the fact that they lived under vastly divergent political, economic, social, and cultural circumstances. This is why Pan-Africanism transcended all geographical barriers which separated these people and the historical circumstances which had given these people different orientations.

The peoples of Asia were treated by their white rulers more or less in the same way, and the results were the same. A 'consciousness of kind' was generated right across the gigantic continent and resulted in the vigorous emergence of Asian nationalism which in due course effectively liquidated foreign rule over most parts of Asia.

Formulated Pan-Africanism owed its existence to the Negro and African intellectuals. While the desire for things black or African was conceived in the hearts of millions of inarticulate Negro and African masses, the intellectuals saw to it that this desire was carefully analysed, reasoned out, and given the fullest articulation. They gave it direction, and a good programme, and continued to give it full backing until it became a universally recognized force to reckon with. They gave this deep desire, this aspiration in the black soul, a theory which did not fail to move the hearts of those who loved and prized human freedom above everything else, and they gave it a practice that moved many into positive action to realize freedom for the black man.

The history of Pan-Africanism is fairly long and decidedly complex, and we cannot go into it in any detail as our main concern here is not so much Pan-Africanism as African nationalism. Pan-Africanism is a background to our main topic and we shall therefore deal with the question of Pan-Africanism fairly shortly.

It must be clear that Pan-Africanism is a feeling common to peoples of African descent wherever they may be. We may further describe it as a re-awakening of the African spirit in relation to itself and to the world at large. It is the desire of the African to reassert himself in Africa and abroad. It is a new self-conception of the African peoples. Pan-Africanism is a reaction of the African to the white supremacy which has for decades relegated him to the realm of fauna and flora. Peter Abraham says:

'Africa? She is a little like a heart. You've seen the shape of her. It's like a heart. Africa is my heart, the heart of all of us who are black. Without her we are nothing; while she is not free we are not men. That is why we must free her, or die. That is how it is.'[1]

Pan-Africanism may be defined as a common identification of the peoples of African descent who have discovered their common destiny and who demand to be treated as equals of men of other races. Fundamentally, Pan-Africanism is a revolt against the doctrine of racial inferiority which centuries of oppression and humiliation have rammed down the throats of the dark-skinned peoples, and is a reaffirmation of the equality of the dark-skinned peoples with the peoples of any race.

The history of Pan-Africanism began with the Pan-African Conference which was convened in London in 1900 under the chairmanship of Sylvester-Williams of the West Indies. Delegates who attended this Conference were Negroes mainly from England, the West Indies, and the United States. The aim of the Conference was to arouse British responsible opinion to protect natives in African lands from abuses. The question of independence was not raised at this Conference, although DuBois who was also present suggested self-government for the colonies. In 1919 the First Pan-African Congress was held in Paris. The delegates petitioned the Allied Powers to place former German colonies under international supervision. The second Pan-African Congress was held in 1921 in London, Brussels, and Paris; the Third in 1923 in London and Lisbon; and the Fourth Congress in 1927 in New York.

It is noteworthy that in all these Congresses it was the American and West Indian Negroes who took the lead. The dominant theme was a plea for humane and just treatment for the colonial peoples. The question of independence or self-government usually did not come up, and if and when it came up it was soon smothered by its then seeming far-fetchedness. It was not until the Fifth Congress which convened in Manchester in 1945 that African leaders like Kwame Nkrumah, Jomo Kenyatta, Peter Abrahams, and others took the initiative and related the deliberations of the Congress to the concrete situation in Africa. This Congress adopted the following declaration:

[1] Peter Abraham, *A Wreath for Udomo*, Faber & Faber, London, 1956, p. 57.

We affirm the right of all colonial peoples to control their own destiny. All colonies must be free from all foreign imperialist control whether political or economic. The peoples of the colonies must have the right to elect their own governments, without restrictions from foreign powers. We say to the peoples of the colonies that they must fight for these ends by all the means at their disposal . . . the struggle for political power by colonial and subject peoples is the first step towards, and the necessary prerequisite to complete social, economic, and political emancipation . . . your weapons—the strike and the boycott—are invincible. . . . Today there is only one road to effective action—the organization of the masses. And in that organization the educated colonials must join. Colonial and subject peoples of the world, unite.[1]

Here we see Pan-Africanism take a new turn altogether. Previously, it had followed the path of reform, but now it was treading on the path of take-over politics. It was no longer reformist politics. This militancy was to be felt all over Africa for the next twenty years as we shall see at a later stage of this book.

The next milestone of Pan-Africanism was the 1958 All-African Peoples' Conference held in Ghana in December. The Conference of Independent African States which had been held in April 1958 to forge 'closer links of friendship, brotherhood, co-operation, and solidarity' among the independent states of Africa, was attended by only eight independent African states, but the All-African Peoples' Conference was attended by delegates from the non-independent African countries who came from Southern Rhodesia, Northern Rhodesia (Zambia), Nyasaland (Malawi), South Africa, Tanganyika, Kenya, Mozambique, Angola, and some West African countries. The delegates who attended this Conference for the first time had their eyes open as to what it meant to be an independent African country and as to how they could also fight for the independence of their respective countries. When they returned home the African nationalist movement received a new impetus. 'Freedom now!' and 'One man one vote!' became the magic words at African political rallies. Ghana, as the first black country to receive independence from a colonial power, inspired the delegates.

To strengthen Pan-Africanism, Prime Minister Kwame Nkrumah, who had inspired so many delegates, later established the Kwame Nkrumah Ideological Institute at Winneba, which was initially designed to project the concept of the 'African Personality' which

[1] George Padmore, *Pan-Africanism or Communism? The Coming Struggle for Africa*, New York (Dennis Dobson, London, 1956), pp. 171–2.

the 1958 All-African Peoples' Conference had enthusiastically endorsed. I had the opportunity of visiting the Institute in 1961. I was left with the impression that here was an institution trying to teach people who had for decades been taught that they were nothing, to think African, to dream African, to act African, to feel African, to live African. It was the declared aim of the Institute to give the African a new conception of himself—to be proud that he was African, and not to be apologetic about it. It was the aim of the Institute to encourage the African to hold up his head among men of other nations and races, and no people can go forward in this world unless they take themselves seriously, and they cannot command the respect of other nations and races unless they can hold their own. This is what the Kwame Nkrumah Ideological Institute had stood for. Only a people with sufficient self-pride can make the grade as a nation.

In 1962, a three-month course on 'positive action' and the philosophy of the 'African Personality' was held at the Institute, and students from Angola, Mozambique, Portuguese Guinea, Cape Verde Islands, Southern Rhodesia, Northern Rhodesia (Zambia), Zanzibar, Basutoland, Bechuanaland, and Swaziland attended the course. Their vision of a free and independent Africa became clearer. They acquired a more definite sense of direction which sent them back to their homelands with new fires of freedom burning in their breasts.

But in spite of Pan-Africanism's vision of a free Africa and of a United States of Africa to which all African peoples belonged, regional and local fears, jealousies, shortcomings, and lack of foresight have prevented Pan-Africanism from achieving some of its important goals. While it has largely succeeded in achieving its goal of an emancipated Africa, it has failed to realize its goal of a United States of Africa; but as a political philosophy it still grips the imagination of African political and nationalist leaders. It has also succeeded in realizing loose economic federations on a regional rather than on a continental scale.

The Conference of Heads of States in Addis Ababa from 22 to 25 May 1963 was yet another strong expression of Pan-Africanism on a governmental level. Thirty-three Independent African States, represented by their Heads, attended this Conference which resulted in the creation of the present body—the Organization of African Unity—which has swallowed up the Freedom Movement of East, Central, and South Africa (PAFMECSA), and the Casablanca and Monrovia groupings which, though divided, had been expressions of Pan-Africanism. African nationalists from non-independent

African countries took full advantage of this illustrious Conference which they besieged with their freedom petitions. The author was among these besiegers. United as we were in our belief that non-independent Africa should attain independence as soon as possible, and that it was the duty of the independent African states to help the non-independent ones to this end, we (1) reaffirmed our support of African nationalists in Rhodesia; (2) reiterated our concern for South-West Africa, whose cause we should support before the International Court of Justice; (3) recommended that efforts be made to establish common action fronts; (4) recommended that training be given in all sectors to nationalists from liberation movements; and (5) recommended that a body of volunteers be promoted to assist African liberation movements.

This, briefly, is the course Pan-Africanism took from 1900, at the time of its first conference in London, when it was still much nearer to being an intellectual exercise concerning itself with remote ideas, to 1963, when direct confrontation in decolonizing Africa was openly advocated. The Summit Conference of the Independent States of Africa which met in Cairo in 1964 harped on the same theme of decolonizing Africa at a more accelerated pace. The conferences held in Accra (1965), Addis Ababa (1966), and Kinshasa (1967) devised procedures by which independent African States could more effectively assist in the liquidation of colonialism and settlerism. A special Committee for Liberation was established at the first O.A.U. (Organization of African Unity) conference in Addis Ababa in 1963. It has since become the most important Committee of the O.A.U. It is charged with the responsibility of collecting and distributing material and financial support for liberation movements. The concept of liberation is a recent but novel addition to methods employed in the interest of African nationalism. For a people to be a nation they must withstand, willingly and with determination, all the obstacles in their national life. If colonialism and/or settlerism stands in our path, it must be resisted and removed. In fact, its removal becomes an important dimension in our new nationhood. When the countries of Europe were threatened by Nazism, they came to the same conclusion, otherwise they would have been absorbed by it.

Philosophically viewed, Pan-Africanism and African nationalism are the reverse sides of the same coin. Whether local nationalism will finally surrender the fruits of her victories over colonialism to Pan-Africanism in order to bring about the United States of Africa which is the ultimate vision of Pan-Africanism remains to be seen.

CHAPTER 8

The African Himself

Up to this point I have not tried to paint the picture of the African in his pre-European days. I have confined my attention exclusively to external forces that stimulated, formulated, and shaped African nationalism. In this chapter I wish to answer the following questions: did the African have any sense of freedom before the coming of white people to Africa? Did he treasure freedom? Was he prepared to defend it once it was potentially or actually threatened? Did the African have any democratic institutions before the European era?

Many Westerners have argued again and again that freedom was introduced to Africa by the white man; that democracy was also European-introduced; that the African clamour for freedom and for democracy was but a clamour for 'the things of the white man'. My main task therefore is to try to determine the presence or absence of freedom and democracy before white people came to Africa. My leading questions are: Are freedom and democracy indigenous or alien to Africa? Was the African struggle for independence something that was there before or after European occupation?

To answer these questions it is proposed to examine broadly some of the most important areas of African life—namely, philology, the institution of slavery, African history, and lastly, African legislature and judicature, both of which we shall also discuss elsewhere.

African linguistics, even on a most superficial level, yields information that throws more light on the investigation. The following table will illustrate our point more clearly:

English	freedom
French	liberté
Portuguese	liberdade
Latin	libertas
Spanish	libertad
Zulu (South Africa)	inkululeko
Xhosa (South Africa)	inkululeko
Ndebele (Rhodesia)	inkululeko
Shona (Rhodesia)	rusununguko
Sotho (Lesotho)	tokoloho

Ibo (Nigeria)	efe
Ga (Ghana)	henoyeli
Ewe (Ghana)	vovome
Twi (Ghana)	fawohodie
Swahili (East Africa)	uhuru
Nyanja (Malawi)	ufulu

If we examine the institution of slavery, the following table is impressive:

English	slave	slavery
French	esclave	esclavage
Portuguese	escravo	escravatura
Latin	mancipium	servitus
Spanish	esclavo	esclavitud
Zulu	isigqili	ubugqili
Xhosa	isigqini	ubugqini
Ndebele	isigqili	ubugqili
Shona	nhapwa	nhapwo
Sotho	lekhoba	bokhoba
Amharic (Ethiopia)	baria	barnet
Ibo	oru	igba-oru
Ga	nyon	—
Ewe	amefele	kluwinyenye
Twi	donko	—

The chief interest here is not philology as such but what light these philological data throw on the present investigation into the existence or non-existence of freedom among the African peoples before the advent of white people. From these two tables it is apparent that there is no linguistic resemblance between African and European words. The African words are as un-European as the European words are un-African. There is no actual philological relationship between the European and African words. The logical conclusion therefore is that the concept of freedom was not foreign but indigenous to Africa. To the best of my knowledge of African philology in general, and Bantu philology in particular, there is hardly an African language that has no word or phrase for 'freedom' and 'slavery'.

But the existence of the word 'freedom' in the African languages cited so far is by no means conclusive evidence that freedom was an accomplished fact among the African people. The philological existence of freedom and slavery could be equated with that of a fairy or goblin. Do these words arise out of the exuberance of imagination or out of real-life situations? In other words, have these words an historical or merely a fictitious content?

It is common historical knowledge that slavery existed in Africa long before white people came. The existence of two classes of people—namely, the captor and the captured, master and slave—logically implies that of freedom and unfreedom. If slavery was known to Africa before the coming of the white people to Africa it follows that freedom was also known to Africa. Slavery is the deprivation of human freedom. Where there is no freedom there cannot be slavery. Both freedom and slavery flourished within an historical *milieu* and not within the realm of fiction. This point is useful as it throws more light on the fact that the African struggle for independence has its roots in the pre-European Africa, and African languages are a living testimony to this fact.

I shall now turn to African history and see what information substantiates or refutes the philological fact of the nativeness or non-nativeness of freedom on the continent of Africa. I shall not attempt to cover all African countries. I shall take only a few samples to demonstrate that long before the white people came, there were many bitter, cruel tribal wars which resulted in the subjection of tribes by others, and in the domination of tribes over others. I shall begin with the history of West Africa.

The history of tribal wars in West Africa is a long and complicated one. For a brief survey which gives a rough picture of tribal conflicts there is T. R. Batten's little volume, *Tropical Africa in World History*, Book Three. Here it is possible only to highlight certain historical facts. In the Gold Coast, for instance, there were many tribes that were very hostile to one another. Very often the stronger tribe conquered the weaker tribe and deprived it of its freedom. As time went on the subject tribe would try to regain its lost independence by making an open revolt against the conquering tribe. Sometimes the conquered tribe sought the help of another strong tribe so that it would be able to overthrow the domination of the victor tribe, and thus regain its lost independence. The life-and-death struggle between the Ashanti and Fanti is a good case in point. As the independence of the Fanti was constantly threatened by the Ashanti the Fanti sought European protection to preserve their tribal integrity against the Ashanti. Incidentally, such foreign protection turned out, in the long run, to be foreign domination. The same tribal struggles existed among the Yoruba and other tribes of Nigeria.

The history of the Bantu-speaking peoples south of the equator reveals the same struggle between victor and vanquished tribes. In Zululand, for instance, there arose at the beginning of the last century a black military genius by the name of Shaka. Sometimes this African military genius has been called the 'Black Napoleon of South Africa'. He conquered many small tribes and made them into one Zulu nation. Then he embarked on a grand scheme of conquest. Other tribes whose sovereignty he threatened unsuccessfully attacked him. Seeing that they could not live in complete freedom and independence while Shaka threatened them with subjection, death, and extinction, they trekked into the unknown where they hoped to live in peace and complete freedom, and thus began the early nineteenth-century migrations of the Bantu-speaking peoples. The Angoni fled from Shaka's fury and settled in what is now Nyasaland. The Shangana fled from Zululand and settled in what is now Portuguese East Africa. The Ndebele crossed the Drakensberg Mountains, and settled temporarily in what is now called the Transvaal, but harassed here by the Boers, they crossed Rudyard Kipling's 'great, grey-green, greasy Limpopo River' and settled in what is now Southern Rhodesia. The Mantati fled westwards and attacked the Bechuana, and later turned south against the Griqua, and after thorough defeat by the latter, fled northwards and settled in the neighbourhood of the Victoria Falls on the Zambezi River. These were the Makololo later found here by Dr. David Livingstone.

The reader should note these points so that he may understand better the trend of African nationalism. The African tribes subjected one another; that is, deprived one another of freedom long before the white people made their influence felt on the whole continent of Africa. The tribe so subjected tried more often than not to win back their freedom. They did this by rising against the conqueror, or by joining hands against the conqueror, and if this was not feasible the subject tribes or the tribes threatened with subjection fled from the conqueror to reassert their independence elsewhere. Their hearts, as they fled from the conqueror, panted and throbbed with the desire for freedom—independence. Freedom was not therefore only philologically but also historically known to Africa. The northward and westward flights of the Bantu-speaking tribes from Zululand can be compared with the general exodus of the peoples of Europe to America in the seventeenth and eighteenth centuries. European peoples were running away from tyranny at home, and the Bantu tribes were running away from Shaka's tyranny in Zululand. The European people wanted to found new settlements in the new world where they could be free. And so did the African tribes want to found new settlements where they could be free. The African struggle for independence began long before the white man came to Africa.

The coming of European powers to Africa had certain important results. It liberated the weaker tribes from the actual or potential domination of the stronger tribes. It gave real protection to these weaker tribes, and it is common historical knowledge that many African tribes, fearful of their more powerful neighbours, often sought European protection. The European conquest of many parts of Africa therefore brought a considerable measure of independence and protection to many African tribes, but it also brought the master tribes, so to speak, under immediate European domination. Both the victor and the vanquished became subjects of European powers. To begin with, this alien domination was a great relief to the once-subject tribes. It compensated for the freedom that had been lost to the ruling tribes. But this alien domination was a thorn in the flesh of the once-master tribes. We can make this point clear by quoting what some Africans used to say during World War II when asked whether they would like to be under German rule. They said, 'It makes no difference to us to be under British or German rule. In both cases, it's foreign domination,' and secretly many of these Africans wished Germany success so that the European powers in Africa might have first-hand experience of what it feels like to live under foreign domination. In the same way the subject tribes were only too happy to see their former masters become subjects of aliens. In fact, European powers used many of these subject tribes to conquer ruling tribes.

The new European administration which was based on military strength made no distinction between the once-ruler and the once-ruled. All tribes were treated in the same way. The once-ruling tribes resented being placed on an equal footing with the once-subject tribes, and the subject tribes which had helped the European powers in conquest of the ruling tribes were equally disappointed that the new European administration which they had helped to set up did not give them preferential treatment. It regarded them all as a 'bunch of natives'. This greatly helped in bringing together the hitherto hostile tribes and they soon united against the new common enemy.

Another important point that must be discussed, before proceeding to trace the African efforts to regain their lost independence, is that of the parcelling out of Africa to European powers. When Africa was finally mapped out large movements of tribes became illegal. Before the acquisition of Africa by Europeans, if a tribe felt that it could not overthrow the ruling tribe, or that it could not defend itself against the threatening tribes, the whole tribe trekked to some other parts of the territory where it could dwell in peace and freedom. But this became impossible after the occupation of Africa. Clear political boundaries hedged them in, and above their heads loomed foreign domination so that they could not go elsewhere to reassert their independence. They were compelled to fight for it where they were. Solution by trekking to the north or to the south was no longer possible.

Many Westerners have contended that Africans were perfectly happy under European rule, and that the struggle against European rule was due to an educated African minority that was power-hungry. We wish to address ourselves to this part of the problem, and to do this we shall have to rely on history, for there is no other way of demonstrating the truth or the untruth that Africans wanted to be ruled by European powers. The historical struggle to regain their lost independence or to remove European threats to their independence can be better appreciated by following the moves which different tribes made from time to time. Among the historical items listed in the Ghana independence souvenir of 6 March 1957 were the following highlights:

1817 British Mission to Ashanti.
1821 British Government took control and placed British settlements under the Sierra Leone Government.
1824 British defeated by Ashanti.
    Governor Sir Charles McCarthy killed.
1826 Ashanti defeated at Dodowa.
1873 Ashanti army defeated at Elmina.
1900 Ashanti besieged Kumasi but defeated.

The history of South Africa also affords many examples of the unwillingness of African tribes to fall under European rule. The well-known 'Kaffir Wars' between the European settlers and the Xhosa throw more light on how African tribes from time to time endeavoured to guard their integrity against foreign invaders.

In what is now Rhodesia similar uprisings occurred. In 1896 the Matebele rose against the British with the hope of regaining their independence but failed to do so. In the same year the Mashona also made an unsuccessful revolt. They were quelled by British guns. As recently as 1952, the Kikuyu, who formed the bulk of the Mau Mau movement, made an attempt to regain their lost independence, which they eventually did on 12 December 1963.

This is enough to show that the present European rule in Africa has, in many places, been established by European military force, and whatever acquiescence the African showed in the European rule, it was not out of design or intention but out of necessity. In every instance where the African has tried to regain his lost independence European guns have quickly swung into action, and have spoken for European domination against African freedom. In the end the African lost faith in his spear ever bringing him his freedom, which he had lost to Europeans whose guns had proved too strong for him. So for a while he developed a philosophy of indifference and tried to make the best out of a bad job. But even his newly acquired philosophical indifference did not extinguish the spark of freedom in his heart. His heart yearned for the freedom which is the birthright of every human being, so he tried to organize himself peacefully since he had failed otherwise, that eventually he might regain his lost freedom. This brings us to another aspect of our discussion.

There have been too many African political organizations to go into in a work of this nature. We shall only pick out a few representative examples here and there to demonstrate that the African struggle for freedom, having failed to achieve its goal through military action, had to change its tactics. African political movements indicate sufficiently the African's desire for freedom in the land of his birth. These movements may have worded their aims and objectives in different ways, and they may have employed different methods in achieving these aims and objectives, yet they have all had one thing in common—the regaining of their lost freedom.

All the African political organizations emerged as the result of the Africans' failure to regain their freedom by military action, and as a result of the African's love for freedom. These African political organizations were trapped and crippled from time to time by adverse European legislation which was deliberately directed towards rendering them ineffective as organs of securing African political freedom. But despite all this, these organizations did not lose sight of their main objective—African freedom.

The Bantu Congress of South Africa, the forerunner of the African National Congress of South Africa, began in 1912. This Congress came about as the result of the Act of Union of Cape Colony, Natal, Orange Free State, and the Transvaal in 1910, 'which made it plain that the African was not to be accepted as a citizen in the Union. Race and colour were to be absolute and permanent criteria by which to assess human worth.'[1] This further threat to the freedom of the African soon united the once hostile tribes, and hence Zulu, Xhosa, Sotho, Shangane, and Venda sank their tribal identities and joined hands as African people who stood against the African-downgrading European rule.

In 1913 the Government of the Union of South Africa passed a Land Act introducing rural residential segregation. To combat this obnoxious Act the Congress raised the necessary funds, and in 1914 despatched a strong and representative deputation to England to plead for the African cause, but the deputation failed. Despite strong Government opposition the Congress was active. In 1952 it organized passive resistance against all discriminatory legislation in South Africa, and this landed in jail thousands of Africans who were prepared to buy freedom through suffering; but the Government was too strong for the Congress. It damped down the African resistance to its own will. The Congress was later banned. The Pan-Africanist Congress which was very militant was also banned.

The late leader of the South African National Congress, Chief Albert Luthuli, was restricted to his home almost indefinitely. Mr. Robert Sobukwe was banished to Robben Island after serving a three-year jail sentence.

The Gold Coast (now Ghana) also affords a good study of African political movements aiming at securing freedom for the African people. The United Gold Coast Convention came into existence for the purpose of securing African political freedom. In 1949, however, this political organization was succeeded by the newly formed Convention People's Party, and it was this Party which swept Dr. Kwame Nkrumah into power in 1951, and it was this Party which was responsible for the creation of the new independent State of Ghana (6 March 1957). Its motto right from the beginning was 'Self-government now'.

At the beginning of this chapter, this question was asked: Did African people, before the coming of the white people to Africa, have any conception of freedom? Philologically, the existence of freedom before the coming of white people to Africa has been demonstrated. I have also shown historically how the African

[1] *Africa South*, Oct.–Dec. 1956, p. 71.

struggled to regain and maintain his independence before and after European occupation of Africa. The African struggle for independence is as old as the European struggle for independence. In short the concept of political freedom is as native to Africa as the native African himself. The European powers succeeded temporarily in suppressing the African's desire for independence, but, to quote Sigmund Freud, in the unconscious the suppressed wish still exists, only waiting for its chance to become active. African nationalism, as we have stated elsewhere, was the European-suppressed African's desire to rule themselves, reasserting itself against hostile circumstances. In the struggle for their independence Africans were and are not fighting for 'the things of the white man' but for their things which the white man, to put it bluntly, stole away from them.

Mr. Basil Davidson, British author and journalist, was right when he wrote in *Report on Southern Africa* in 1952:

Today, many people talk of the need for Europeans to make concessions and gestures which will help win confidence in European leadership. But the African does not ask for concessions, nor need gestures of European generosity. He is not asking for privileges. The African is asking for his rights. He seeks to establish equality of all individuals, black, brown, or white. In this demand there can be no half-way compromise, for it is either absolute equality or superiority of one over the other.[1]

There could be no equality between black and white while the European alone held effective power; nor could there be any equality while both black and white jointly and equally held this power since the European was in the minority and the African in the majority. The minority had to be dislodged from power-control in the sole interest of the majority. It is only under majority control that black, white, and brown can enjoy equality as citizens or individuals.

[1] Basil Davidson, *Report on Southern Africa*, Jonathan Cape Ltd., London 1952, pp. 71-2.

CHAPTER 9

The Christian Church

The last two chapters discussed white supremacy as one of the major factors in the rise of African nationalism and the subject will be discussed further in Part 3. This chapter will survey the role the Christian Church has played in the forging of African nationalism on the anvil of history. It will attempt to assess the influence the Christian Church has exercised on the minds, attitudes, and outlook of the African people who have had direct contact with it. The statistical method cannot be of much help here since it cannot help measure those subtle changes which become responsible for great things. Spiritual realities defy any mathematical manipulation, and for this reason in the course of the survey outstanding events and individuals will be singled out to exemplify in what ways the Christian Church has influenced the African people.

Let it be noted right from the outset that when the missionaries went to Africa, they had not the slightest idea of helping African nationalism as such. Their primary goal was to propagate the gospel of Christ to their fellow human beings, although it was not uncommon that some of them were more interested in the propagation of their own particular culture rather than the gospel of Christ. The Church has only been a blind instrument in the whole process of African nationalism. On the whole, missionaries in Asia and Africa have been accused, and not without cause, of standing in the way of African and Asian nationalism. In the main they have been staunch supporters of colonial rule so that colonial powers cannot blame the rise of African nationalism on the missionaries as a class. Our survey will, however, show that missionaries have been unwittingly helpful to the rise of African nationalism.

To appreciate fully the part that the Christian Church has taken in the development of the gigantic continent of Africa it will be well to recapitulate some of the basic historical facts about Africa.

Before the coming of the missionaries to Africa there were only four out of more than 700 different languages which had a native script of their own. The four that had a written form were the Ethiopian Amharic, the Arabic, the Berber Tamachek, and the Liberian Vai. Although the other languages had a highly developed grammar and syntax, they were only oral. So, before the coming of the Christian Church, Africa was cursed with illiteracy (she still is, to a lesser degree, since definite steps are being taken by most of the independent African countries, with the co-operation of international bodies, to wipe out all illiteracy). When the missionaries came, great strides were made in the field of literacy. It is estimated that from 15 to 20 per cent. of the African population can now read and write with varying degrees of proficiency. African literacy is on the increase. There is everywhere in Africa an unprecedented hunger for education and literature. Even uneducated African parents try to make sure that their children get the opportunity they themselves never had. Schools ranging from the dilapidated pole-and-mud hut to the most up-to-date school building are steadily increasing in the bush, farm, town, and city, but the pace is rather too slow for the feverish desire 'to get an education'.

As in American history it is common to talk of the Californian Gold Rush of 1849, so there is an African 'education rush' of the twentieth century. The Christian Church has introduced a new spirit of learning without which no nation can have a truly balanced progress. It is this creative spirit that helped to sustain African nationalism and without which the whole idea would end in dismal failure.

Since the coming of the missionaries to Africa the whole Bible has been translated into more than forty languages; the New Testament into more than eighty; and between 200 and 300 African languages have been reduced to writing. What is the actual relevance of the Bible or the New Testament to African nationalism? We need not elaborate that the Bible has most powerful ideas for the heart and the mind. No man can be brought up on the Bible and remain uninfluenced by it. If it is true that the teachings of the Holy Bible greatly helped in the shaping of European thought, the same thing could be said of Africa. If it is true that the United States owes much to the Bible the same thing could be said of Africa.

One of the unique teachings of the Bible, especially of the New Testament, is the worth and dignity of the individual in the sight of God, and there is a relation between this teaching and African nationalism. According to the African tradition, at least in some parts if not in the whole of Africa, the individual counted in so far as he was part and parcel of the group, outside of which he lost his real worth. In actual practice, this meant that no individual could follow his natural bent beyond the group. All new schemes, new adventures, new thoughts, and new outlooks on life were subject to the approval or disapproval of the group. The individual, to all practical intent, was dominated by the fear of the group, let alone the fear that comes from ignorance, superstitious beliefs, and belief in the existence of evil spirits. Individual initiative had been crippled, but now the African individual was delivered from these fears. The individual was invested with new status, and so it was that these new Christian individuals ventured beyond the confines of their groups, and in many cases these groups in turn looked upon the new individuals as their real saviours. The Bible redeemed the African individual from the power of superstition, individuality-crushing tradition, witchcraft, and other reactionary forces. The same Bible helped the African individual to reassert himself above colonial powers! It is inconceivable to a logical mind that the Bible could deliver the African from traditional domination without at the same time redeeming him from colonial domination. If the Bible teaches that the individual is unique, of infinite worth before God, colonialism in many respects said just the opposite, so that biblical teachings were at variance with colonialism, and it became only a matter of time before one ousted the other. The Bible-liberated African reasserted himself not only over tribal but also over colonial authority.

Two South African Africans were arguing one day on the unhealthy South African situation. One was inclined to censure the whole missionary enterprise in Africa in this strain: 'You see, the missionary came here and said, "Let us pray", and we closed our eyes, and when we responded, "Amen" at the end of his prayer, we found the Bible in our hands, but lo! our land had gone!'

To which the other replied, 'When Europeans took our country we fought them with our spears, but they defeated us because they had better weapons and so colonial power was set up much against our wishes. But lo! the missionary came in time and laid explosives under colonialism. The Bible is now doing what we could not do with our spears.'

African nationalism was strongly influenced by Christian principles. Gandhi, who was responsible for the liquidation of British imperialism in India, admitted, though himself a professed Hindu, that Christ's Sermon on the Mount had greatly influenced him. The Reverend Martin Luther King, the Negro civil rights leader in Alabama, U.S.A., said in his article, 'Non-violence and Racial Justice':

The method of non-violence is based on the conviction that the universe is on the side of justice. It is this deep faith in the future that causes the non-violent resister to accept suffering without retaliation. He knows that in his struggle for justice he has cosmic companionship. This belief that God is on the side of truth and justice comes down to us from the long tradition of our Christian faith.[1]

The above quotation, drawn from the American scene, becomes more enlightening when compared with the African scene. The South African 'Treason Case', which placed 156 Africans, Europeans, and Asiatics under arrest, revealed the influence of the Christian principles on the South African situation. Mr. George Houser, in his article, 'Treason in South Africa?' wrote about those in jail:

The rededication sermon was conducted in the Fort 'Prison'. Chief Luthuli's brief speech closed with the challenge, 'If there are any present who are sorry to be in the Fort and regret their membership in the [African National] Congress has brought them to this pass, let them drop out of the circle. Only those of us who are determined to continue the struggle may sing "Mayibuye" [the Freedom Song] "Let Africa Return".' Everyone sang. Chaplain Gawe led in prayer. The sermon ended with the singing of the African national anthem, 'Nkosi sikelela Afrika'—God Bless Africa.[2]

But it was not only the African Christian who stood against those forces which denied him freedom. True European Christians also stood on the side of what was right—namely, that oppression of other human beings was wrong. What went on in colonial Africa shocked the Christian conscience of both black and white so that, in a real sense, white supremacy found itself engaged in a life-and-death struggle of Christian principles. The Anglican Church of South Africa, for instance, took an uncompromising position on apartheid policy. When the Nationalist Government of the Union of South Africa introduced the new Native Laws Amendment Bill (1957) which would bar interracial gatherings of any kind, the late Archbishop Clayton, in collaboration with four other Anglican bishops, wrote to the Prime Minister stressing the official position of the Anglican Church, which is the second largest denomination in the country:

The Church cannot recognize the right of an official of the secular government to determine whether or where a member of the Church of any race (who is not serving a sentence which restricts his freedom

[1] *Christian Century*, 6 February 1957.
[2] ibid., 6 March 1957.

of movement) shall discharge his religious duty of participation in public worship, or to give instructions to the minister of any congregation as to whom he shall admit to membership of the congregation.

Further, the constitution of the Church of the Province of South Africa provides for the synodical government of the Church. In such synods, bishops, priests and laymen are represented without distinction of race or colour. Clause 29(c) makes the holding of such synods dependent on the permission of the Minister of Native Affairs.[1]

Bishop Vernon Inman of Natal, South Africa, said, 'As a Church we loathe and abominate the devilish device known as apartheid, and we believe it is leading our country to ultimate ruin. . . . We continue to oppose it as unchristian and we emphasize that it is unSouth African. . . . I imagine not even a heathen would suppose that God would even tolerate apartheid in his own house.'[2]

It was not only the Anglican Church that battled against racial discrimination, but also such denominations as the Methodist, the Roman Catholic, the Congregational, and the Salvation Army. This was not only true of South Africa but of such countries as the then Federation of Rhodesia and Nyasaland, the then British East Africa, and other African countries where Christian Churches and Christian Councils fought for ordinary human justice for Africans.

We have had to quote at length in order to show that the Christian Church has created in Africa, or at least in some parts of it, a strong Christian consciousness that transcends the usual barriers of race and colour, and this Christian consciousness is based on the love of God and the love of our fellow men. It is based on the strong sense of human justice. The story of African nationalism would be incomplete if this Christian awareness was ignored, since it is this awareness that is an integral part of the creativeness of African nationalism. The strength of this Christian consciousness was even demonstrated by the African Christians in Kenya who remained obdurate in the face of Mau Mau terrorism. They chose to suffer and die rather than repudiate their Christian principles which were much disliked by the Mau Mau liberators.

Of course, the non-Christians also support this movement, but while African nationalism was strongly motivated by African consciousness of an oppressed people seeking freedom, Christian consciousness helped it to its feet and imbued it with self-sustaining creativity. The Christian faith may be regarded in one sense as its spiritual father and in another as its guardian angel, whether or not

[1] *Natal Mercury*, 9 March 1957.   [2] ibid.

the Church recognizes these roles. Practically all important African political leaders went through the Christian church school. The African politician may turn his nose up in derision, and twist his lips by way of deprecation when he hears it said that the Christian Church laid secure political foundations for African nationalism, but that need not surprise us, for two reasons. First, as Brutus said in *Julius Caesar:*

> But 'tis a common proof,
> That lowliness is young ambition's ladder,
> Whereto the climber upward turns his face;
> But when he once attains the upmost round,
> He then unto the ladder turns his back,
> Looks in the clouds, scorning the base degrees
> By which he did ascend.

And second, a few missionaries working in a colonial atmosphere also adopted a colonial attitude towards the African and stood between him and his big dream of independence. The few erring missionaries should not however be confused with the main stream of missionaries who, by example and precept, demonstrated the reality of the Christian principles. The fact is that the Christian faith is like a prolific fruit tree whose fruit gives life to those who care and those who do not care for it. Christian and non-Christian Africans have reaped in varying degrees the blessings of the Christian faith, and this is as it should be since God himself sends rain on the just and the unjust.

About 25,000,000 Africans profess the Christian faith. The Christian Church has replaced, in many parts of Africa, the otherwise exclusive clan or tribal worship to which only the members of the clan or tribe went. Members of different clans and tribes worship together. There now exists among the different clans and tribes of Africa religious communication. The Church has helped the religious unification of many parts of Africa. In many places tribal consciousness is being pushed into the background, and Christian consciousness has given people a wider horizon.

Christian schools have played an important part in the lives of African people. The average African educational curriculum included the European language spoken by the administering colonial power, one African language, religious instruction, arithmetic, history, geography, physical training, singing, physiology and hygiene, and nature study. On the practical side it included woodwork, vegetable gardening, poultry, animal husbandry, brickmaking, forestry, and general manual work. Girls learned sewing, laundry, and house-keeping. On the recreational side, it included athletics, soccer, basket ball, volley ball, and baseball. The extra-curriculum included girl guides (girl scouts), boy scouts, debates, drama, and variety shows.

After elementary education some girls and boys trained as teachers. The teacher-training curriculum consisted of child study, teaching methods, school organization, practical teaching, and other subjects incidental to the teaching profession. Other school-leavers trained as medical orderlies and nurses. In addition to these professional schools, there were also schools where boys trained as builders, carpenters, agricultural demonstrators, and forestrymen. In most cases these artisans turned out very good work by any standards.

The study in African schools of European, English, and American, as well as African history, has had a profound influence upon the African people. The European struggle for liberty, for religious toleration, for freedom of thought and expression, and European resistance against tyranny thrilled the African students. How often have my history students requested me to tell them about certain historical figures! 'Please, sir, tell us about that tenacious English bulldog' (Sir Winston Churchill). 'Please, sir, tell us more about Martin Luther and his ninety-five theses. Oh, that man! He was a man!' 'Mahatma Gandhi's soul was more powerful than the British Navy and the Royal Air Force put together.' 'Tell us, please, about the Boston Tea Party.' 'David Livingstone, the man who stopped the slave trade in Central Africa.' 'Please tell us about Mr. Govern-ment-of-the-people-by-the-people-and-for-the-people' (Abraham Lincoln). European, American, and Indian heroism thrilled African students. They admired the firm stand against tyranny. But sooner or later the African admirer sought to overthrow the tyranny of his Euro-pean hero. Perhaps the following account will make the point clear.

Historical incidents were twisted to give them an African flavour. The famous American dictum 'No taxation without representation' sometimes ran 'No racial peace without African representation'. The American song 'John Brown's body' was changed when Dr. Kwame Nkrumah was jailed by the then British administration to 'Kwame Nkrumah's body amoulderin' in the jail, But his soul goes marching out.'

When the student spokesman had finished presenting students' grievances to the principal of one mission school in Southern Rhodesia, in the midst of a tense atmosphere of over 400 students, he bowed stiffly to the principal and concluded, 'Sir, we thought it was right and proper that this matter should be brought before you in this fashion so that government of the students, by the students, for the students shall not perish from this mission station.'

Abraham Lincoln's Gettysburg address had been taught to these students for the sheer beauty of its prose. It had been taught to improve the students' oral English—the rising and falling inflection, clear enunciation, and good choice of simple powerful words—but it had turned out also to be a handy political weapon!

The Reverend E. T. J. Nemapare of Southern Rhodesia broke away from the Methodist Church in Southern Rhodesia and established an indigenous Church of his own. He was seriously accused of 'breaking the body of Christ' and in his defence he stated, 'No Protestant has any right to accuse me of breaking the body of Christ. It is my Protestant right to protest, and I don't see what's wrong with exercising my birthright.' He remained unmoved and went ahead with his indigenous Church. The Reverend Nemapare had been taught Church history during the course of his evangelistic training. The curriculum had been drawn up by the Church officials, but the interpretation of its contents was entirely his own.

Africans found themselves confronted by European colonial powers. Africans wanted to understand how the control of Africa had slipped from the hands of its rightful owners, and therefore they studied European history long after they left school. They then studied how the control of Africa could be restored to its rightful owners, and so they studied liberation movements—that is, movements overthrowing an imposed rule like the English Revolution of 1688, the American Revolutionary War of 1776, the French Revolution of 1789, and the Russian Revolutions of 1917. They wanted to understand how other people got their independence so that they might also get theirs. They were not so much interested in pure as in applied knowledge. 'Other people did it. Why can't we?' they often asked themselves after the lessons of history had thoroughly convinced them that they had much in common with other peoples of the world. The African freedom salute 'Mayibuye!'—Let Africa return—pointed out clearly that Africans in general believed that Africa had gone away from them, and it also showed the Africans' strong belief that Africa would one day return to her rightful owners.

Kwame Nkrumah's reading-list may perhaps give substance to what has been stated. Dr. Kwame Nkrumah said in his autobiography:

I devoted much energy to the study of revolutionaries and their methods. Those who interested me most were Hannibal, Cromwell, Napoleon, Lenin, Mazzini, Gandhi, Mussolini, and Hitler. I found much of value to be gleaned, and many ideas that were useful to me later in my own campaign against imperialism.

At first I could not understand how Gandhi's philosophy of non-violence could possibly be effective. It seemed to me to be utterly feeble and without hope of success. The solution of the colonial problem as I saw it at that time lay in armed rebellion. How is it possible, I asked myself, for a revolution to succeed without arms or ammunition ? After months of studying Gandhi's policy and watching its effect, I began to see that when backed by a strong political organization it could be the solution to the colonial problem. In Jawaharlal Nehru's rise to power I recognized the success of one who, pledged to socialism, was able to interpret Gandhi's philosophy in practical terms.[1]

The study of history placed very powerful weapons in the hands of many Africans, and historical consciousness was one of the chief factors behind African nationalism. The educated African was gaining ideas and ideologies that were highly dangerous to colonialism.

The study of European languages usually consisted of reading, oral, grammar, dictation, spelling, essay-writing, letter-writing, comprehension exercises, and general European literature. On the Junior and Senior Cambridge, or Matriculation level, as well as University level, African students followed exactly the same English syllabus as the one followed by English-speaking students. The examinations given were the same, and diplomas awarded were the same. The study of European languages had aroused such a keen interest among Africans that at times it bordered on fanaticism. No African considered himself modern and well educated unless he had mastered some European language. There was nothing new in this. During the Hellenistic period those who could not speak the Greek language were deprecatingly called barbarians, not cultured. With the ascendancy of Rome, Latin became the learned man's language, and later, French became every cultured man's language. The conquered tend to copy the language and customs of the conqueror. Just as many leading Indians had been brought up on English literature, so many leading Africans in British Africa had been brought up on the same English syllabus. This fact was also true of French

[1] Kwame Nkrumah, *Ghana: Autobiography*, Thomas Nelson & Sons Ltd., Edinburgh and London, 1956, pp. xiii–xiv.

and Portuguese Africa. Such African professional men as lawyers, teachers, doctors, journalists, parliamentarians, and accountants carry on their work in some European language common in Africa. And so European languages are now understood and spoken in many parts of Africa, not only by the five million Europeans there, but also by at least 70 million Africans. In other words, the church schools in Portuguese, British, and French Africa brought European languages to the African people.

The medley of African languages—over 700 of them—has already been mentioned. This has been held as one of the factors responsible for the countless divisions found all over Africa. The various tribal groups had been walled off from one another not only by geographical barriers, but also by language difficulties. Linguistically, an African from the Republic of South Africa was as much a foreigner to an African from Kenya as an English-speaking American would be to a Russian or German. Even Africans within the same country were linguistic foreigners to one another since one country might have more than one language. In Rhodesia, for instance, there are two main native languages which make one section regard the other as foreigners. It is estimated that there are 250 different tribes in Nigeria, and that each tribe has its own language, although for practical purposes these are sometimes reduced to 20. At present it is common to talk of only three major languages of Nigeria, namely, Yoruba, Ibo, and Hausa. These groups occupy the three major regions of the country. In Liberia, with a population of about 2½ million people, there are about 20 native languages. In South Africa there are about five major native languages spoken by about 11 million Africans. This could be said of any other African country. An African observer once said, 'Language divisions have made the white man to thrive very well in Africa. The day these close up, the white man will have to change his techniques.'

One of the results of the study of European languages was the breakdown of these linguistic walls. I met in the U.S.A. Africans from Ghana, Nigeria, Liberia, Sierra Leone, the Republic of South Africa, Kenya, Tanganyika, Uganda, and Ethiopia and, but for the English language we all learnt at school, we would have remained foreigners to one another. As soon as we met we felt quite at home because we were able to communicate with one another. One English-speaking African is perfectly at home with another English-speaking African from any other part of Africa. The same thing is true of Portuguese-speaking and French-speaking Africans. A common language is very useful in the forming and shaping of the common destinies of peoples of diverse backgrounds. While we do not pretend that all Africans in former British, French, and Portuguese Africa could all speak English, French, and Portuguese respectively, we want to make it clear that while in African tribe A only 10 per cent. might speak English, the same thing might be true of tribes B, C, D, E, F, G, and the like, so that communication through the medium of English was carried on among these literate members of A, B, C, D, E, F, and G, and the result was an exchange of ideas, thoughts, aspirations, plans, and frustrations, and these were interpreted into the vernacular for the benefit of the illiterate masses so that even the illiterate became more enlightened by the study of European languages. The Africans say, 'You can learn the tricks of a man by learning his language.'

The Christian Church, by sending religious, educational, and industrial missionaries to Africa broadened the outlook of many an African. It provided opportunities for many Africans to develop their latent qualities; it has discouraged tribal hatred and encouraged universal brotherhood instead. Incidentally, tribalism was also discouraged by African nationalism when it emerged so that, in this respect, the Christian Church paved the way of the universalism—that is, the non-tribalness—inherent in the African nationalism that was to come. The present enlightened African political leadership would be next to impossible but for the Christian Church that spread literacy to many parts of Africa.

CHAPTER 10

Colonialism's Positive Role

Up to this point colonialism has not been credited with the emergence of African nationalism. An examination of the forces that were at work in the shaping of African nationalism would be incomplete if the positive role of colonialism was ignored altogether. The major areas wherein colonialism brought real progress to the peoples of Africa will therefore be studied. But, let it be understood right from the beginning, the discontinuance and destruction of colonialism on the continent of Africa are not regretted, even though it had a certain positive role. To most Africans colonialism meant the deprivation of their freedom by European powers.

As the scramble for Africa caused a great deal of confusion and unnecessary toe-treading among European powers, it became necessary that the spheres of influence be formally defined. Prince Bismarck, for the Imperial German Government, therefore invited interested powers to what is now known as the Berlin Conference of 1884. Among other things stipulated in the Berlin Act of 1885, the result of this Conference, were freedom of trade for all nations, suppression of the slave-trade, the civilizing of the natives of Africa as well as their evangelization, protection of religious, scientific, and charitable institutions, and the preservation of law, order, and peace.[1]

This Act threw Africa open to more missionaries, explorers, traders, scientists, and new institutions since it guaranteed protection, good order, and peace. One of the blessings of the advent of European powers in Africa was the suppression of slavery and the slave-trade. The gigantic wave of humanitarianism that was sweeping across the whole continent of Europe coincided with European expansion to Africa. The abolition of slavery in Africa was one of the practical expressions of this European humanitarianism. The very provisions of the Berlin Act produced one of the paradoxes of history, which can be summarized thus—the acquisition of African land and the civilization of the African. Land acquisition, in the course of events, turned out to be imperialism, and civilizing the African turned out to be the liquidation of that imperialism.

[1] T. W. Wallbank, op. cit., pp. 108–9.

What did the European powers mean when they asserted that they wanted to civilize the native of Africa ? In European terms one thing remains clear: to civilize a primitive people means, among other things, to bridge the gap between the civilized and the uncivilized. In other words, to bring the primitive man to the level of the civilized man. The logical conclusion of the civilizer and the civilized becoming equals is just as inescapable as that of the training of boys and girls who eventually become colleagues of their professors. If then the Berlin Conference was motivated by purely imperialistic designs in the opening up of Africa, history cheated the European powers in that the rise of African nationalism directly challenged European imperialism. It should be remembered that in many ways European imperialism in Africa gave to African nationalism unprecedented strength. If, on the other hand, the Berlin Conference was motivated by a genuine spirit of wishing to civilize the African natives, then the European powers achieved their main object in the rise of African nationalism, since it became the desire of the African people to reach the same level as the European powers who set out to civilize them.

With the passing away of slavery, slaves were accorded new human status. Let it be noted in passing that the general outlook of a slave on life is different from that of a free man. His potential capacities are crippled, stunted, and pushed into the background. The emancipation of slaves therefore opened a new world to thousands upon thousands of African slaves; hence, it can rightly be said that European colonial powers, by dealing slavery a deathblow, set the whole continent of Africa on a new venture of freedom and human dignity.

The advent of European powers in Africa not only saw slavery coming to an end, but also the terrible tribal wars. What are now the Republic of South Africa, Rhodesia, Nigeria, Ghana, Portuguese, and French-speaking Africa were torn with countless tribal wars so that the chief occupation of most able-bodied African men was that of raiding other tribes. Europe itself was of course a war-torn, war-cursed country. But the European powers, whose weapons were superior to those of the Africans, were able to impose peace on the African people, and this was to the general good of the peoples of Africa. Something more creative took the place of destructive tribal wars. It is obvious, however, that with the European dictator of peace at the top, the African soon gained peace and good order but lost the control of his country. The European powers, although they had failed to keep peace in Europe, were soon regarded by most native tribes as 'peace-makers', bearers of 'deeds of humanity', and 'bringers of enlightenment'. Indeed, it has been rightly asserted by both Africans and Europeans that the European occupation of Africa, although it deprived people of their independence, helped to direct the minds and activities of the native peoples away from destructive to constructive programmes of action.

When European powers came to Africa their immediate objects were trade, mining, and farming. They had come strictly for business. As more European settlers came, more European villages, towns, and later cities, sprang up and towered above natural vegetation. Mines for gold, diamonds, chrome, asbestos, copper, and uranium were opened, and to these thousands, and later millions, of Africans flocked to work. For the first time the African went into the bowels of the earth. There he drilled holes into the hard rock, and was an eyewitness to 'things that split rocks, and sent pieces of rock flying into the air'. It was overpowering, overwhelming, and all-exciting. The novelty of it all continued for quite some time. 'Wonders have come,' the Africans used to say again and again as they reflected on these new experiences. In the towns and cities many Africans were employed as domestic servants, factory workers, and general labourers. Many joined the police force. On the farm many saw new agricultural implements and entirely new methods of farming. Thousands of Africans were employed in the construction of roads, railroads, bridges, and dams. Many Africans began learning new Western skills so that today you get armies of Africans who drive taxis, trains, cranes, and tractors. African builders and carpenters have come to stay. There is, without doubt, a general wave of Westernization sweeping throughout the continent of Africa, and this has had, in general, beneficial effects on the people.

Volumes could be written on the good things that European powers brought to Africa, but this is outside the scope of this book. The reader should note these four things, among others, that the coming of the European power, brought to Africa: the coming together of different tribes; better communications; a new economic system; and the creation of new classes among the African people.

With the coming of mines, towns, and cities the different tribes of Africa found themselves thrown together. Tribesmen who had never had anything to do with one another, found themselves living together in one area, working side by side with one another, and the need to get along with one another became imperative. For instance, in the Johannesburg gold-mines members of tribes from the whole of South and Central Africa, and even East Africa, are to be found in large numbers. Rhodesia is full of African labourers from Zambia, Malawi, Tanzania, and neighbouring territories. With the coming together of these tribes, the horizons of many Africans were greatly extended. Just as the U.S.A. was popularly regarded as the melting-pot of the nations, so also was every mine, town, and city in Africa a melting-pot of the tribes. Many Africans who have been thus urbanized, early learned that what counted in the long run was not belonging to this or that tribe, but rather, to use the Ndebele phrase—to *sebenza nzima*—to work hard. Eventually the African regarded himself not so much as a tribesman; but as a worker. A common language, a kind of *lingua franca*, soon developed, and thus communication was facilitated among members of different tribes. Down in the mine, in the factories, in the police force, in domestic service, on the farm, in the store, hospital, clinic, and a host of other European-introduced institutions and occupations, no tribal barriers existed or were encouraged. People just mixed freely. Tribalism among urbanized Africans was on its way out, and something else was taking its place. It was estimated in 1957 that over 40,000,000 Africans had left the tribal régime and had been caught up in the industrial system. In the Belgian Congo it was estimated that just under 3,000,000 Africans had become urbanized to some extent. In short, every year saw more Africans drawn from their tribal set-ups, and every year saw the ranks of detribalized Africans swell. While the Christian Church and schools were exploding colonialism, colonialism, by its aggressive economic programme, was busy exploding tribalism, and in collaboration with Church and school the job could not have been done better or faster. African tribalism was on the way out as a result of the onslaught of industrialism, and the handwriting on the wall read, 'From tribalism—what next? Of course, African nationalism.'

It must be remembered that fundamentally the tribal concept arose out of a common need of a group of a people who had a common goal. Since this common need was no longer there, and since a new era of common interests had been created by the colonization of Africa, a new common goal was formulated and nationalism was the expression of that goal. The Government of the Republic of South Africa is now trying to push back the African tribes into their former tribal patterns to avert this so-called danger of African nationalism which is an amalgamation of different tribes with a common objective.

Colonial powers have helped with the detribalization of the African, and the African in many cases had to be detribalized before he could aspire nationally. There was then a growing tendency among the Africans to think of themselves less and less as tribesmen, but more and more as Africans. The different tribes of Nigeria began to regard themselves more and more as Nigerians, in Ghana as Ghanaians, in Tanzania as Tanzanians. This point will be made clearer when we take up in the next chapter the question of African political consciousness as evidenced by African political institutions.

With the construction of good roads, bridges, and railroads, and with the introduction of motor-cars, lorries, buses, trains, and aeroplanes, the African people have become highly mobile. Mobility of the population has greatly accelerated the exchange of ideas. The dissemination of all kinds of information has been unprecedented in African history. Even illiterate people are now better educated and better trained than ever before. Radio and, more recently, television have revolutionized African outlooks. Different parts of Africa and, indeed, the world, have now been brought to the very doors of the radio-owning African. With the rise of literacy African populations have become a vital reading public and the press has appeared. Africans read not only their own thoughts but those of others separated by vast stretches of water. What happens in Europe, Asia, America, and Australasia has become of real interest to the African people.

It is seen, then, that colonialism has created a radio-audience and a television-audience. It has created a reading public. It has created a press-writing and reading public. It has created a travelling-public by land, sea, and air. All these four kinds of African public are still growing every year. The tendency has been the creation of a comparatively well-informed and enlightened African public, and a focussing of the world's problems on the public consciousness of the African people. The African public that existed before the introduction of the radio, the press, the train, and the motor-car was highly localized. Particularism is now in many places giving way to universalism. Colonialism gave birth to a new brand of African, a non-tribal African: in short, a national African.

The tendency of a radio, press-writing, reading, and travelling public is to encourage the habit of building knowledge, comparing things and people, following ideas, and passing judgement. Men begin to judge themselves by the higher standards of others. If they find themselves wanting, they determine to improve themselves. The whole Westernization of African people is a good illustration of this point. Colonialism engendered a vigorous spirit of progressive competition in all walks of life, and this is part of the legacy that colonialism had bequeathed to Africa.

The economy of the peoples of Africa should now be studied. In most areas the only medium of exchange was barter. There was no money economy to speak of. But now a new economic system has been introduced. Millions no longer have to own livestock for their subsistence. They can sell their labour, and this new moneyed class is very powerful. One African Malawian once put it, 'Today all people do not need to have goats, cattle, and sheep in order to live. They only need money. If they have money, why, they have cattle, goats, and sheep in their purses. Money is the cow that does not move, breathe, drink, and eat grass. It is a very good cow. You can milk it any time. You can eat and drink it any time. It is a cow that does many things for us.' This represents a complete mental revolution; more so when it is borne in mind that this is the attitude of a man who never saw the four corners of a classroom. Millions of Africans now have bank accounts, and millions are taking out insurance policies, and this represents a growing confidence in banking institutions and insurance companies. A capitalistic class is growing among the African people. The African public is becoming more and more aware of the new ways of investing money.

The last of the four points raised is the new social and economic stratification of the African peoples. New armies of African bakers, butchers, cobblers, tailors, storekeepers, clerks, mechanics, builders, carpenters, and a chain of others have made their appearance on the scene, and they are changing the whole African social pattern. In relation to industry and commerce, the African acquired class consciousness as a worker. He wanted his voice to be heard in industry and commerce. The birth of African trade unions was really that of the new African who believed in economic justice and who was prepared to fight lawfully to achieve this end. European trade unionism has been transferred to the African scene; but African workers as a class were painfully aware of the glaring discrepancies between European and African wages. Their bone of contention was that their economic reward was far below that of a European wage-earner. The African worker felt a deep sense of economic exploitation. Alan Paton described the feelings of John Kumalo thus:

Here in Johannesburg it is the mines, he said, everything is the mines. These high buildings, this wonderful City Hall, this beautiful Parktown with its beautiful houses, all this is built with the gold from the mines. This wonderful hospital for Europeans, the biggest hospital south of the Equator, it is built with the gold from the mines.

There was a change in his voice, it became louder like the voice of a bull or a lion. Go to our hospital, he said, and see our people lying on the floors. They lie so close you cannot step over them. But it is they who dig the gold. For three shillings a day. We come from the Transkei, and from Basutoland, and from Bechuanaland, and from Swaziland, and from Zululand. And from Ndotsheni also. We live in the compounds, we must leave our wives and families behind. And when the new gold is found, it is not we who will get more for our labour. It is the white man's shares that will rise, and you will read it in all the papers. They go mad when new gold is found. They bring more of us to live in the compounds, to dig under the ground for three shillings a day. They do not think, here is a chance to pay more for our labour. They think only, here is a chance to build a bigger house and buy a bigger car. It is important to find gold, they say, for all South Africa is built on the mines.

He growled, and his voice grew deep, it was like thunder that was rolling. But it is not built on the mines, he said, it is built on our backs, on our sweat, on our labour. Every factory, every theatre, every beautiful house, they are all built by us.[1]

It has been seen that colonialism gave to Africa a new vigorous industrial pattern, a new social and industrial consciousness, a new way of organizing and doing things, new skills, new insights, new dreams and visions. It created a new climate, a new environment. It annihilated many tribal, linguistic, ethnic barriers and divisions. It was largely responsible for the unification of African tribes, where previously tribal divisions had made for weakness rather than for strength. It brought Africa into international light, and this was very helpful if Africa was to keep pace with the rest of the world. Since colonialism fertilized, stimulated, invigorated, and shaped African nationalism, it is understandable when African observers say, 'The twentieth-century African nationalism is indeed the child of European colonialism be it within or outside wedlock.'

[1] Alan Paton, *Cry, the Beloved Country*, Jonathan Cape, London, 1948, pp. 36–7.

CHAPTER 11

The Nationalist Methods

If all the dimensions of African nationalism are to be understood, the methods that African nationalism employed to achieve its objectives should be examined. Broadly speaking, there are two methods that African nationalism employed, and still employs, in trying to realize its aspiration: non-violence, and violence. Before discussing each method, some observations should be made.

It is one of the characteristics of human nature to follow the method of trial and error. Men tend to employ methods that yield dividends. They discard those methods which do not show results. History has many illustrious examples.

The Stuart kings are an example. The great power formula of the Stuart kings was the divine right of kings. According to this formula God had appointed a particular form of government, and whoever was king, it was assumed, had been appointed by God's will. Accordingly, the king was responsible to God alone for his conduct of national affairs. He was not responsible to the people who were expected to obey the king. Disobedience to the king, rebellion against him, and any unbecoming behaviour toward the king was considered not only as a crime against the king but as a sin against God. The people had no right to depose the king however harsh, tyrannical, and foolish his rule might be. The king was above Parliament which was responsible to him, and he to God alone. (In fairness it must be pointed out that it was not only the Stuart kings who believed in the divine right of kings: Roman emperors and the popes are other examples.)

The English tried to reverse this doctrine which worked to their disadvantage. They tried to do this peacefully without resorting to open warfare between themselves and their kings, but they failed to bring the kings under the law like everybody else. A bitter struggle between the Crown and Parliament began, and this developed into an open warfare which resulted in the beheading of King Charles I. This taught the future kings of England that they were responsible to Parliament, and not to God alone as Charles I had claimed by virtue of the divine right of kings. If Charles I had heeded the claims of Parliament, the violence which finally broke out and cost him his head could have been avoided.

The French Revolution provides good parallels which may throw more light on the logic of the methods African nationalists used. Southgate summarized the causes of the French Revolution in the following words:

Many causes combined to bring about the great uprising of the French people in the year 1789. The peasants, except a few in the east and north-east of France, were no longer serfs, but they lived in a state of extreme poverty and misery. Their depressed condition was due to the backward state of agriculture and to the weight of the taxes and dues which they were called upon to pay. The nobles were much more numerous in France than in England, and included men who in this country [England] would be regarded merely as country squires. They were exempt from most of the taxation and from compulsory military service, which were burdens borne only by the peasants. They possessed privileges which were denied to the lower orders. They alone were permitted to hunt and fish, and to keep doves and shoot; they levied tolls on the roads and in the market-places, and they possessed authority to enforce in their courts the obligations of the peasants who lived on their estates. The villagers were compelled to grind their corn at the lord's mill, to press their grapes in his wine-press, to kill their cattle in his slaughter-house, and to bake their bread in his oven, and they had to pay dues to him whenever mill or wine-press or slaughter-house or oven was used.[1]

When those who were thus oppressed—representing the unprivileged merchants, professional men, farmers, and labourers, numbering about 26,000,000 people in all—rose against 400,000 nobles who fiercely clung to their privileges without giving in even an inch, the result was the open clash between the millions of the have-nots and the few haves which resulted in what history has come to identify as the French Revolution. Although it first sought the limitation of the royal veto, thereby eliminating absolute monarchy and replacing it with limited monarchy, this movement resulted in the complete downfall of the monarchy as an institution, and in the rise of republicanism. It is worth noting here again that after repeated petitions by the French commonalty for social, judicial, and political reforms which met the blank wall of privilege, the people soon learned that the 'petition' method did not yield the expected and

[1] George W. Southgate, *European History 1789–1960*, J. M. Dent and Sons Ltd., London, 1963, p. 1.

desired dividends. Revolutionary forces broke loose and bloodshed took its course.

A look at the Russian revolt of 1917 will throw more light on the contention that when one method does not yield the expected and desired results, people will abandon that method and try another until they have got what they want. The struggle in Russia centred around the principle of the Tsar's autocracy. He did everything in his power to muzzle, silence, and destroy any democratic expression. As far back as 1895, the people asked him 'that the voice of the people should be heard' and that the law henceforth be respected and obeyed not only by the nation but also by the ruling authorities. To this request the Tsar had this to say: 'I am aware that in certain zemstvo meetings voices have been lately raised by persons carried away by senseless dreams of the participation of zemstvo representatives in internal government. Let all know that I intend to defend the principle of autocracy as unswervingly as did my father.' The following day an open letter appeared: 'Senseless dreams concerning yourself are no longer possible. If autocracy proclaims itself identical with the omnipotence of bureaucracy, its cause is lost . . . . It digs its own grave . . . . You first began the struggle, and the struggle will come.'

Since the Tsar did not heed the demands of the people for democracy, there was no alternative but to move away from the 'petition' method to another that would give the people what they wanted. In February 1917 (according to the old Russian Calendar, but March according to the Western Calendar) a revolution took place and overthrew Russian tsardom with violence and blood. Autocracy had come to an end, and democracy had begun.

In all three revolutions we have instanced two factors stand out and seem to decide what method was to be followed in each case. The interplay between these two factors resulted in the kind of method used to solve the problem. The first one of these was the constantly expressed grievances of the people, and the second was the attitude of those who held the power, and were therefore in a position to redress these grievances. In other words, when those in power ignore the popular demands to right injustice (social, political, judicial, and economic) and people become desperate, revolutionary methods become inevitable and these may develop into 'bloody' methods. Those in power are in a strong position to influence the type of method to be used in solving the serious problems facing the people. The willingness or unwillingness of the rulers to face up to the realities of the grievances of the people they rule determine the method the people use in getting a redress. In the three revolutionary cases we have briefly discussed it was the unwillingness of the kings that encouraged the revolutionary and violent method. The divine right would not yield to the demands of parliament; the privileged orders of France stuck stubbornly to the brotherhood of the few against the demands of the brotherhood of the many; and tsarism obstinately refused to give a hearing to the popular voice. The American revolutionary wars followed the same pattern. When the British Parliament failed to face up to the realities of their American colonies bloodshed was the result.

Too often the critics of African nationalism appear to think that the African nationalist is a fundamentally different species of mankind, overlooking that whatever methods African nationalists have used in their grim struggle for independence, these have been largely determined by the realities of the prevailing situation in which they found themselves. Like other races, African nationalists have used methods which they calculated would work under the circumstances. Non-violence will be discussed first.

Under this broad principle we may specify five-sub-principles. These are the principles which we have distilled from the actual workings of non-violence in many parts of Africa.

1. *The Constitutional Approach:* This principle presupposes a constitutional arrangement which allows African political participation in some form or another. The question of a constitutional approach by the African nationalists, for instance, did not arise in South Africa where the African people were denied the vote. The question of working outside the constitution does not arise for people who have no constitutional rights! It is a contradiction not only in terms but in fact to accuse people who are ignored by the constitution of being unconstitutional in their acts! In what was the Belgian Congo, for example, the African nationalists could not use the constitutional approach since the Belgians tolerated no politics in their colonies. In Angola, Mozambique, and Portuguese Guinea no constitutional arrangements had been made for possible African participation. In French North Africa, French Equatorial Africa, and French West Africa constitutional arrangements had been made, although they were unsatisfactory in that African representatives sat in the National Assembly in Paris instead of in their respective countries. Because of this constitutional arrangement the African nationalists in French Equatorial Africa and French West Africa

peacefully pursued their legitimate political claims and got their independence without violence (this was not true of North Africa which we shall discuss later on in this chapter).

In such British protectorates as Bechuanaland, Swaziland, and Basutoland where constitutional arrangements looked forward to an African majority government taking over, African nationalists pressed only for constitutional reforms without resorting to violence. The same was true of Ghana, and Nigeria followed more or less the same pattern. Tanganyika got her independence without any violence. In short where there was constitutional hope of ending white rule, the African nationalists stuck strictly to the principle of the constitutional approach.

2. *Parliamentary Participation:* Where constitutional arrangements were satisfactory, the African nationalists participated in the various legislative bodies. In what was Northern Rhodesia, now Zambia, a limited number of Africans sat in the Legislative Council since there was such an arrangement. What was then Nyasaland, now Malawi, also had Africans in the Legislative Council. The now defunct Federation of Rhodesia and Nyasaland also allowed African participation in the Federal Assembly. The same could be said of Tanganyika, Kenya, and Uganda. But when it occurred that these arrangements (which were usually loaded against the African) were intended in fact to entrench white rule with a semblance of African participation, the Africans in many cases withdrew their participation, and African nationalists soon demanded the boycott of such. So it was that in due course no African nationalists participated in the legislative assemblies of Northern Rhodesia, Nyasaland, the Federation of Rhodesia and Nyasaland, and Southern Rhodesia. In other countries, however, this principle of parliamentary participation was adhered to until the countries concerned became fully independent. Very often African nationalists considered these legislative bodies as the cooling chambers of African nationalism.

3. *Extra-Parliamentary Pressure:* This principle was often resorted to when the second principle was found not to yield the expected results. The African nationalists usually organized mass rallies throughout the country. At these mass rallies people were taught to shout chosen slogans. For instance, in the Gold Coast, now Ghana, the people shouted such slogans as 'Self-government now!' and 'Freedom now!' In Nyasaland they shouted '*Kwacha!*' (Dawn); '*Sitifuna Chitanganya!*' '*Chitanganya ngachipite!*' (We don't want Federation! Federation must go!). They also shouted,

'Self-government!' 'Kwacha' became a magic word not only in Nyasaland but also in Northern Rhodesia and Southern Rhodesia. It penetrated into the remotest areas of Central Africa. In Northern Rhodesia 'Kwacha!' and 'Freedom now!' were shouted with the same gusto. In Southern Rhodesia, 'Freedom now!' 'Izwe Lethu!' 'Nyika yedu!' and 'Majority rule now!' were repeated at most rallies. In Tanganyika, Kenya, and Uganda 'Uhuru!' (Freedom) and 'Uhuru na Umoja!' (Freedom and Unity!) were powerful mass slogans.

At these mass rallies the African nationalists took every opportunity to detail eloquently the oppression of white rule. They reminded the land-hungry millions how they had been uprooted from the land, and how landlessness had been forced upon them to make room for white farmers, every one of whom had many thousands of acres of land. In cities they reminded the people of the blatant colour bar which subjected African people to untold indignities and humiliations; they reminded the people of low wages and unsatisfactory working conditions and poor African housing; they reminded the Africans of the high wages paid to European workers, the better working conditions and better housing for European workers. The nationalist orators were quick to link up these unsatisfactory conditions with European rule which had to go if matters were to be improved for the good of the African masses. The nationalist orators, at the height of their orations, jeered, ridiculed, sneered, castigated, minimized, and discredited European rule, poured venom on it, and ignited the dynamite fuses which in due course exploded and destroyed it. From these mass rallies the African nationalists emerged the true leaders of the people and the people returned to their homes fully charged with the spirit of freedom and with their hearts burning with a new fanatic zeal to free themselves.

The real aim of this approach—extra-parliamentary pressure— was to cause the masses to become more aware of their miserable plight, to know the cause of their miserable lot, and to kindle in their hearts the confidence and faith that they could remove the cause if only they united against that cause. It was believed that if such unity could be brought to bear on the powers-that-were, the desired result could be achieved. This approach made terrific gains, but only under such circumstances that the powers-that-were were sufficiently alive to the legitimate grievances and aspirations of the people and were ready and willing to make the necessary redresses, constitutional and otherwise.

4. *Appeal to Public Conscience:* The African nationalists used everything at their disposal to gain the sympathy of the European public. This they did by writing well-reasoned arguments advancing their cause, but it became clear to the African nationalists that although there were many European liberals who were in favour of drastic constitutional changes, many of these European liberals could not go all the way with African nationalists who demanded 'One man one vote now'. While they felt that the black man had a genuine case against white rule, none the less they had their serious reservations when it came to handing over the reins of government to the black man; and this reservation on the part of the European liberals became indistinguishable from progressive conservatism, which held tenaciously to the view that the white man must continue to rule the black man, but must rule the African justly. This was a diametrically opposite view to that of the African nationalists who were working for a complete take-over. In any case the appeal to public conscience could only succeed if such a 'white conscience' was sufficiently sensitive to the morality of right and wrong; but since white supremacy was its own morality accountable only to itself, this principle was not much followed by African nationalists who soon dismissed it, saying, 'It's unreasonable to expect white settlers or *colons* to campaign for their liquidation. Our appeal must be directed to the African public conscience. African nationalism must anchor in the African conscience, not in the European conscience.' This distinction, as later events were to prove, was not without reason.

Some European liberals pointed out sincerely but mistakenly that passive resistance was an important political instrument which had been successfully used in India. This method had appealed to the British public conscience, and the European liberals urged the use of this weapon to stir up the conscience of Europeans living in Africa who were in control of all effective political power. The African nationalists, however, were quick to point out that the India situation was quite different from the one in Africa and therefore the magic formula of Mahatma Gandhi's passive resistance could not yield the desired results. First, passive resistance as a political instrument aimed to arouse the British public conscience. It presupposed the existence of such a conscience. Secondly, the Indian philosophy of life was one of negating, not affirming life. Physically, religiously, and philosophically, the Indian was in a position to effect passive resistance through the calculated violence of the then British administrators. In Africa, however, the British public conscience was not the deciding factor. It was not there. The white settlers and the *colons* did not have this British conscience. They had only a 'white supremacy' conscience highly insensitive to the legitimate demands of the African peoples. Secondly, the African peoples had a fundamentally different philosophical orientation. Theirs was not one of negating life, but one that affirmed life. Their blood was too warm to respond passively to the severe lashes of colonialism and imperialism. In South Africa, the African nationalists tried passive resistance in 1952, and instead of arousing the conscience of the whites there, bullets were used to break all passive resistance. The ghastly firing on the peaceful African demonstrators at Sharpeville in 1960, resulting in the immediate death of over seventy passive resisters, is too well known to need any comment. In Southern Rhodesia, Northern Rhodesia, and Nyasaland passive resistance was tried but failed to yield the expected results. Passive resistance failed in these countries, while it succeeded in India, because the conditions that obtained in India did not obtain in Africa, and, while history is popularly supposed to repeat itself, in fact it never does.

5. *Appeal to International Conscience:* This principle has already been discussed in our description of the influence of the United Nations on African nationalism. African nationalism did everything in its power to arouse international conscience, and this effort has been largely successful for many parts of Africa.

* * *

Where non-violence failed, African nationalists resorted to violence. Before this method is examined, the following observations should be made.

Violence as a method of liberation presupposed that there was no other channel open to the demands of the people. It was only resorted to as a desperate measure. Where white people refused to give constitutional recognition to popular demands violence did take place, but it should be remembered that it was not violence for its own sake, but as a means of forcing the powers-that-were to give in to popular demands. We are here not concerned with the question whether violence was good or bad. In any case African nationalists were concerned with what worked, with what was effective. Whenever and wherever people are engaged in a power struggle the methods they resort to are only determined by the question: how much effect have the methods? never by: how right are such methods?

The African nationalists did not follow the path of idealism, but that of realism, and realism in such cases meant what worked. After all, if the powers-that-were used any means to deny the people of their rights in the land of their birth, was it not the realistic thing to do to employ any effective method to establish the rights of the people in their own country? Was it morally right that the Africans were treated as non-citizens in their own country? Did the white man hold Africa on moral grounds? Did he not hold Africa on the basis of brute force? Was brute force sensitive to the peaceful pleas and implorings of morality? These questions do indicate that the problem of having to decide about non-violence is not as easy as some people seem to think. The deciding factor between using the method of non-violence and that of violence is its effectiveness in a given set of circumstances.

In consideration of the method of non-violence, there are three methods to bear in mind. First, the unconstitutional method; second, the method of disrupting the economic, the social, and the general life of the country; and third, the method of armed revolt. These three methods were widely used in the emancipation of many African countries just as they were used in the liberation of the continent of Asia.

1. *The Unconstitutional Method:* Strictly speaking, the unconstitutional method was not one of violence, but a preliminary exercise to it. This method presupposed that the powers-that-were were not prepared to sit at a constitutional conference with the African nationalists and hammer out a constitutional arrangement which would be acceptable to the African people. In other words where there was no constitutional channel to right the wrongs that oppressed the people, the African nationalists resorted to the unconstitutional method. This meant defying those laws which were oppressive in their very nature and often such defiance resulted in a head-on collision between the African nationalists and the forces of so-called law and order, and violence became inevitable. Mass demonstrations against oppressive laws often resulted in riots as a result of police intervention.

2. *The Disruptive Method:* This consisted of disrupting the economy of the country with a view to forcing the powers-that-were to come to terms with African nationalism. Boycotts and strikes which began on a non-violent basis ended in violence when they broke out into looting, stoning vehicles, and committing other acts of destruction. Cutting telephone wires, road-blocking, blowing up bridges and

installations were often resorted to. Destruction of crops and live-stock on European farms and such government installations as dip-tanks and government rest houses in rural areas was another means.

3. *The Method of Armed Revolt:* This method was used princi-pally in those countries where the powers-that-were remained un-heeding in the face of popular demands. The Kikuyus of Kenya, having come to the conclusion that the white man there was not in any mood to concede African popular demands, resorted to an armed revolt which resulted in the deaths of some 12,000 Africans and about thirty Europeans. For almost five years Kenya faced the grimmest struggle in the liberation of that country. The armed struggle was also resorted to in Algeria since the French *colons* would not give in to popular demands. Bullets, hand grenades, and bombs shattered city, town, village, and house alike. The *colons* were determined that Algeria was to remain French, and the Algerians were equally determined that the Algerians should rule themselves. Only power decides the question of power. The armed struggle went on for seven years. It only ceased when the popular demands had been granted. In Angola the armed revolt began in 1958 and it is still going on. In Mozambique the armed struggle began in 1963, and it is still going on. In Portuguese Guinea, the method of armed revolt has also been used. This illustrates the point that when the powers-that-were refused to come to terms with the popular demands, armed revolt became inevitable. This was not only true of the African nationalists but also true of nationalists of other races, developed and underdeveloped.

PART THREE

The Philosophy of White Supremacy

CHAPTER 12

The Power Formula

Hitler, who sired the Herrenvolk doctrine of the twentieth century, once said, 'It is a sin against all reason, a criminal madness, to train a semi-ape to become a lawyer.'

J. G. Strijdom, the one-time Prime Minister of the Union of South Africa, said in 1953:

Our policy is that the Europeans must stand their ground and must remain Baas [master] in South Africa. If we reject the Herrenvolk idea and the principle that the white man cannot remain Baas, if the franchise is to be extended to the non-Europeans, and if the non-Europeans are given representation and the vote and the non-Europeans are developed on the same basis as the Europeans, how can the European remain Baas? Our view is that in every sphere the European must retain the right to rule the country and to keep it white man's country.

Sir Roy Welensky, Premier of the then Federation of Rhodesia and Nyasaland, bellowed out white supremacy:

It has got to be recognized, once and for all, that when we talk of maintaining high standards in the Federation . . . we mean White standards. People who have in their minds that we might abdicate in ten or fifteen years . . . ought to prepare themselves for a rude shock.[1]

As Edmund Burke observed, 'Those who have been once intoxicated with power even though for one year, can never willingly abandon it.'

White supremacy was regarded as an absolute. It was accountable to itself, and not to anything outside itself. It was an ideology. Its appeal to its adherents is not based on reason, scientific approach, or objective assessment, but on irrationality and emotionalism and subjectivity. White supremacy paid no attention to any scientific observations made by distinguished anthropologists who have found no evidence of the racial superiority presupposed by white supremacy. Franz Boas had this to say:

Our tendency to evaluate an individual according to the picture that we form of the class to which we assign him, although he may not

[1] Patrick Keatley, *The Politics of Partnership*, Penguin Books Ltd, Harmondsworth, 1963, p. 272.

feel any inner connection with that class, is a survival of primitive forms of thought.... Freedom of judgement can be attained only when we learn to estimate an individual according to his own ability and character. Then we shall find, if we were to select the best of mankind, that all races and all nationalities would be represented. Then we shall treasure and cultivate the variety of forms that human thought and activity has taken, and abhor, as leading to complete stagnation, all attempts to impress one pattern of thought upon whole nations or even upon the whole world.[1]

White supremacy was its own justification. Let it be borne in mind that white supremacy had no meaning at all unless it was intended from start to finish as a power formula, and like all power it was indivisible, inalienable. Either the white people ruled, or they didn't. They could not share that power with the African. This power formula was given the name *eurocracy* in another chapter. Now a new power formula, *afrocracy*, has made its appearance in Africa, and like its predecessor it is indivisible, inalienable. This is the true nature of all power. It cannot be shared with foreigners. It can only be shared with and among its citizens. Foreigners can and do become citizens in free Africa.

No African or any other non-European has yet sat in a South African Parliament. The power formula there excluded any African participation in the running of the country.

In what used to be the Federation of Rhodesia and Nyasaland, the power formula gave the appearance that the African was within its orbit when in fact he was outside it. It had been constructed in this manner, first, to appease international criticism, and second, to satisfy the demands of the British Government which had insisted that Africans must be given a measure of political participation in the Federal Government. In a Federal Assembly of fifty-nine members, eighteen represented about 7,000,000 Africans, and the remaining forty-one members represented only 220,000 whites! The principle of deciding issues by majority vote gave way to that of white supremacy, and this phenomenon was repeated, as we shall see shortly, all over European-ruled Africa. In statistical terms, in the Federation of Rhodesia and Nyasaland 3 per cent. of the population was represented by 41 Members of Parliament, and 97 per cent. of the same population by only 18! In other words, 3 per cent. of the

---

[1] Franz Boas, *The Mind of Primitive Man*, The Free Press, New York, (Collier–Macmillan Ltd., London, 1963), pp. 241–2.

population controlled 69.5 per cent. of the Federal seats, and 97 per cent. of the population controlled only 30.5 per cent. of the seats!

The Southern Rhodesia Constitution of 1961 provides for a Legislative Assembly of sixty-five members, fifty of whom are Europeans and fifteen Africans. There are 4,000,000 Africans and 200,000 Whites and about 20,000 Asians and Coloureds in the country. Since the last two racial groupings are not represented separately, we shall here only talk in terms of Africans and Europeans. This means that the Europeans, who represent less than 5 per cent. of the population, have fifty parliamentary representatives and Africans, who represent more than 95 per cent. of the population, have only fifteen representatives. Fewer than 5 per cent. of the population holds 77 per cent. of the seats, and over 95 per cent. of the same population holds only 23 per cent. of the seats in the Legislative Assembly.

Rhodesia has what is called 'qualified' franchise. In theory any one who has the necessary qualifications can register as a voter and therefore can participate in the national elections. White-settler politicians have argued vehemently that this qualified franchise is not based on the colour bar, but on the economic bar, and that this economic bar applies to every adult citizen regardless of the colour of his skin. As will be seen in the next chapter the economic bar, based on racialism, is weighted heavily against the African. There is a dual economic system in Rhodesia—one for Europeans and the other for Africans. The latter operates on the principle of deliberately depressed economy so that only a few Africans can register as voters. Since the black man enjoys numerical strength over the white man, and since it is this numerical strength that counts and which is decisive in any situation of power distribution and control, the white man in Rhodesia has had the political genius of inventing an ingenious political device which in theory repudiates white supremacy, but entrenches it in practice. The genius of Rhodesia's 'qualified franchise' is that it gives the vote to virtually all adult Europeans, but denies the same vote to most African adults. In other words, because the Europeans earn higher wages and salaries, they are able to qualify as voters, but because Africans earn low wages they are unable to qualify in large numbers as voters. Hence what is called qualified franchise in Rhodesia is, in effect, universal adult franchise for the white people, and 'majority-disqualifying franchise' for the African. Even if it is denied that this was the intention of the architects of Rhodesia's qualified franchise, it cannot be denied that this is its effect in full accord with the real intention of white supremacy—namely, that the African throughout Africa shall be held in subjection, and that the white man shall remain in full control of the entire continent of Africa. It is noteworthy that every time the general wage level went up, the voting qualifications also followed suit!

In Tanganyika the same formula was found. The racial representation mechanism there was based on a theory of parity, and in mathematical terms it was a 10-10-10 system for the Legislative Council. Ten Europeans represented about 20,000 whites, ten Africans about 7,000,000 Africans, and ten Asians about 75,000 Asians. This was called equal racial representation. Statistically expressed, the position was this: 98·5 per cent. of the population held ten seats; 1·25 per cent. of the same population ten seats; and ·25 per cent. of the same population ten seats! This is to say, $98·5\% = 33\frac{1}{3}\%$; $1·25\% = 33\frac{1}{3}\%$; $·25\% = 33\frac{1}{3}\%$. It is self-evident that what was called parity was in fact disparity. But the political genius behind this arrangement appears to have been based on the assumption that the Asians who also wanted to dominate the African would invariably vote with the Europeans and thus keep the voting strength of the Africans at the $33\frac{1}{3}$ per cent. level, while that of the Asians and Europeans would be kept at $66\frac{2}{3}$ per cent., and thus keep the power formula intact. Little wonder that the African nationalists there saw through it all and intensified their activities against *eurocracy* and eventually succeeded in having it effectively replaced with *afrocracy*.

So much about Tanganyika. In the Kenya of 1957 there were about 6,000,000 Africans and about 44,000 whites. In the multi-racial government there were only ten African representatives in a Legislative Council of sixty members. These two racial groupings only will be discussed here since, in fact, African nationalism was principally a reaction of the African people to white supremacy rather than to the Asian people, although the whites tried to use the Asian factor to confuse the situation from time to time. The whites were only ·7 per cent. of the population and held forty-five seats while the Africans, who formed 99·3 per cent of the population held only ten seats. In other words, ·7 per cent was equal to forty-five and 99·3 per cent. was equal to ten. (The five seats held by the Asians have been omitted.) The explanation of this glaring anomaly was that in the eyes of white supremacy the African did not count for much. It was therefore left to African nationalism to make the African count for something in his own country.

In all the British Protectorates effective political power was vested in the British Government through the Colonial Office, but the situation in the Portuguese colony of Mozambique is different. In 1926, J. M. da Silva Cunha had stated the Portuguese power position in the following words:

One [idea] is to guarantee the natural and unconditional rights of the native whose tutelage is confided to us . . . and to assure the gradual fulfilment of his moral and legal obligations to work, to be educated, and to improve himself. . . . The other idea is to lead the natives, by means appropriate to their rudimentary civilization . . . to the profitable development of their own activities and to their integration into the life of the colony, which is the extension of the mother country. The natives are not granted, because of the lack of practical application, the rights associated with our own constitutional institutions.[1]

In November 1960, President Americo Thomaz said: 'We are not in Africa . . . like so many others [Colonial powers]. We will continue as always our policy of integration . . . to this end it is necessary for us to be what we have always been, and we will not change.'[2]

Portuguese colonial territories are part and parcel of Portugal herself. Portugal is in Angola-Mozambique, and Angola-Mozambique in Portugal. Portuguese colonial territories therefore do not enjoy any political participation as did the British territories to some extent. The seat of all political power is in Lisbon and there ends the matter, and it remains to African nationalism to turn the scales against this power formula.

What used to be the Belgian Congo also had no political institutions. All political power was based in Brussels. The Belgians, as is noted elsewhere in this book, dominated to serve. That was their power formula.

In French North Africa the French policy of assimilation was in itself a power formula. The Africans had to be French first before they could enjoy full French citizenship. But of course this policy went beyond cultural assimilation. French colonies were regarded as integral parts of metropolitan France. There were no national assemblies in French North Africa, French West Africa, or French Equatorial Africa. The National Assembly was in Paris, and Africans

[1] Quoted in James Duffy, *Portugal in Africa*, Penguin Books Ltd., Harmondsworth, 1963, pp. 163-4.
[2] Quoted in Duffy, op. cit., p. 212.

who represented these colonies did so in Paris. All political power was based in France and there was no thought of handing over the colonies to African rule since these colonies were France and France these colonies. It was left to African nationalism to explode the myth that African colonies were integral parts of France.

CHAPTER 13

The White Supremacy Factor

There is a sense in which 'white supremacy' may be regarded as having been largely responsible for the effective cross-fertilization of African nationalism. Without the existence of this racially based doctrine of 'white supremacy', which adversely affected the African peoples, it is probable that the African peoples would not have sensed so quickly the 'consciousness of kind' which boomeranged on the colonial powers and the white settlers.

What exactly is this 'white supremacy?' It is an assumption that the white man, in relation to the African, holds the highest place in government or power, in economy and society in general. The white man is the highest in the land, and the African the lowest.

An outstanding Rhodesian African politician defined white supremacy as 'the white man's keep-down-the-nigger policy'. A Kenya African defined it as 'the rule-by-might doctrine'. Many African thinkers equate it with Hitler's Aryan doctrine. A Nigerian African once said, 'There are two dangers to the peace of the world—Communism and white supremacy. Both are based on the same principles; both employ the same methods; both aim at the same thing—domination of others.' He went on, 'White supremacy is to us [Africans] as Russian Communism is to Russia's satellite countries.'

An African teacher from Zambia expressed his views thus:

I don't hate white supremacy because it is white. I hate it because it is designed for my domination and humiliation. It hurts me. White supremacy as an avowed European policy presupposes African subjection. The existence of white or black or brown or yellow supremacy implies the suppression, oppression, and exploitation of other people. You don't hear of English supremacy in England, French supremacy in France, or American supremacy in U.S.A., because no Englishman intends dominating other Englishmen, no Frenchman intends dominating other Frenchmen, and no American intends dominating other Americans. But since the white man intends dominating Africa, he talks of white supremacy.

White supremacy is similar to the Hebrew theory of 'a chosen people', and can only survive by presupposing the sub-humanity or human inferiority of other human beings compared with the super-humanity of the white man. One of the barriers preventing and forbidding the development of understanding between black and white was this almost impregnable wall wrought in stone and concrete by white supremacy.

White supremacy produced two groups of people in Africa—the dominator and the dominated. It divided Africa into two hostile camps. The concept of 'consciousness of kind' in the emergence of Pan-Africanism and African nationalism has already been described. The white people were conscious that they ruled as a white group, and the African people also became conscious that they were ruled as an African group. They suffered as a racial group. If there was any racialism at all in African nationalism or in Pan-Africanism it could only have been inspired by the racialism inherent in white supremacy, but that inspired racialism died with the death of white supremacy. Racialism is foreign to the African make-up. It is only characteristic of those who have attained the highest levels of conquest of other human beings. Human races respect each other better outside the highly divisive situation of conqueror and conquered.

Those who dominate tend to hate those who actively resist their domination, and those who are dominated naturally tend to hate those who dominate them. The struggle therefore between black and white was not a racial one engendered by the incidence of blackness and whiteness but rather by the very act of dominating others. It was an open clash between the will of the dominator and that of the dominated of which both Pan-Africanism and African nationalism were but a practical expression. African nationalism was only a practical effort on the part of the dominated millions to throw off the yoke of domination. From the European camp was heard the voice of unflinching determination, 'We dominate to serve,' and from the African camp the thunderous voice, 'Down with white supremacy!' and so the tug-of-war went on throughout the length and breadth of Africa.

The clash between black and white in Africa was one of motive, aim, goal, and purpose. It was a clash of interests, and one of the urgent problems was how to reconcile European interests to those of Africans, and vice versa. It became evident, however, that African interests could not be settled on the terms of the white man since white supremacy was the alpha and omega of European thinking, feeling, and action. White supremacy could not contain the demands and aspirations of African nationalism; nor could African nationalism accede to the claims of white supremacy. A reconciliation between the two was impossible. An effort to reconcile domination and subjection was not only an illogical exercise wasteful of time and energy and money, but an unrealistic and unpractical approach, for what good sense was there ever in hoping that the African would eventually accept the white man's domination and therefore his own subjection?

In Mozambique and Angola, the Portuguese policy is based on the *assimilado* or *civilizado* system. According to this system an African who satisfies certain Portuguese official standards may become assimilated into Portuguese society and virtually become a white Portuguese (except in colour), and enjoy the rights enjoyed by white Portuguese citizens. This is to say, an African can never become a full citizen in Portuguese Africa until he first becomes Portuguese or until he renounces himself first! The whole aim of the Portuguese policy is to prevent the very conception of African nationalism. The African is taught, under the *assimilado* system, to think of himself as a Portuguese in Portugal, not as an African. The Portuguese policy aims at killing the African in the African and at replacing him with a Portuguese. A black-skinned Portuguese seems to be the chief goal of the Portuguese policy.

But the African wants to be himself. He does not like to lose his identity. He wants to be a full citizen of his own country without becoming a poor imitator of the Portuguese; he has no real desire to repudiate his Africanness. An African from Mozambique stated his case well when he said, 'The Portuguese think that it was a mistake on the part of God to make an African African. Their *assimilado* policy is an effort to correct this divine error. However, people like to be themselves and to be accepted as such.'

When I pointed out to him that the Portuguese policy of acceptance was better than that of non-acceptance as in the Rebublic of South Africa, he looked at me rather cynically and with an apparent surprise.

'No,' said he, 'there's no such thing as accepting the African. In Portuguese Africa today there are 1,000,000 who are neither citizens of Portugal nor of Africa.'

'But there are several thousands of Africans who have been assimilated and accepted,' I said.

He laughed scornfully, and then said, as though he was talking to some poor ignorant boy, 'No, my boy. In accepting the several thousands of Africans as you say the Portuguese have done, the

Portuguese are making it appear as though they are accepting the African, when all along they are staunchly refusing to accept him. . . . In accepting the assimilated African, the Portuguese are merely receiving back their own Portuguese they pumped into him. In other words, they are really accepting themselves and not the African.'

I had never thought of it in that way before. I mused over this refreshing thought, and my friend continued, 'You see, it's like saying, "Mr. White Man, you are white and I am black. I shall have to paint you black before I can accept you." This would not be accepting the white man, but my black colour. It's the same thing with us.'

The idea of painting the white man rather tickled me, though his logic impressed me immensely. But my friend was in earnest, and he, perhaps thinking that I had not seen what he was trying to make me see, asked me, 'Do you know why you accept your own baby ?'

'Well, that's my baby, and I'm its father,' I said.

'But suppose you were sure that the baby to whom your wife gave birth was not yours, would you accept the baby ?'

'That would be difficult,' I said.

'Even though the baby came from your wife ?' he asked.

'But the question is not whether it comes from my wife, but from me. And I suppose this holds true for my wife too. If I had a baby by another woman, that baby would not be acceptable to her either,' I said.

'Quite right,' he said eagerly. 'In other words, the baby has to come from both of you to be acceptable to both of you. Neither of you do accept the baby because it is a baby. You accept it because it is part of your flesh and bone.'

'I suppose so,' I said.

'You see what the Portuguese are doing ? They are impregnating the African with their Portuguese, and when the African gives birth to the Portuguese, they accept the Portuguese, not the African. They receive back what they put into the African. The *assimilado* system is a Portuguese refusal to accept the African as he is.'

This argument became more meaningful to me when I remembered that in Rhodesia men and women of African descent receive lower pay, and those of mixed European and African descent receive higher pay, and those of European descent receive the highest pay in the country. The analogy was this, that the Government of Rhodesia, which is almost exclusively white, does not see itself in the pure African and therefore legislates lower pay for Africans. But it is able to see itself more in Euro-Africans and therefore legislates higher pay for this group. The theory that seems to be established by this practice is, 'The nearer to the white skin, the better the treatment. The farther away, the worse the treatment.'

The core of the Portuguese policy is perpetual domination of the African. What has been the result of the Portuguese policy? Certainly, it has not been accepted by the African nationalists from that country. All the African nationalist movements for the liberation of Angola, Mozambique, and Portuguese Guinea have rejected the *assimilado* policy, and they have taken up arms to destroy it and to regain full citizenship in the land of their birth. The Pan-Africanist movement has also set its teeth against the entire Portuguese colonial system.

Closely related to the Portuguese *assimilado* system is the French policy of assimilation. When the *indigène* became civilized and cultured, he became a Frenchman and therefore acceptable to the French society, and full rights of citizenship were extended to him. This system was an attempt to absorb gradually educated Africans, and to include them in the central government of the State. This was quite a realistic policy on the part of the French since it would be bad politics to exclude Africans from all participation in the administration of the country.

But the French system of assimilation had glaring defects since it held the Frenchman or French culture to be the ultimate goal for the African. It created the false impression upon many African minds that there was nothing higher than to be a Frenchman, and many an African resented having to direct all his efforts to becoming a Frenchman some day. The age of subtle pretensions has had its day. The Frenchman could no longer pretend to the African that he was the paragon of excellence deserving his emulation. The African turned away from his French-aroused desire to become a Frenchman. He wanted to remain African and enjoy life to its fullest without being deprived of his rights and privileges on the pretext that he did not look and behave like a Frenchman. African consciousness, which has been pushed into the background by the advent of European powers since the scramble for Africa in the nineteenth century, was now coming irresistibly to the fore.

It is obvious that the French policy, like that of the Portuguese, was inherently one of political domination, and African nationalism, though greatly diluted by the French system of assimilation, was, in

French Africa, the desire to overthrow this domination. The political struggles in French North Africa that resulted in the liberation and full independence of Tunisia, Morocco, and Algeria show that the French system of assimilation had lost its attraction. The Moors and Arabs did not want to be French any more than Frenchmen wanted to be Moors or Arabs.

The Belgian Congo—the then home of 15,000,000 blacks and 115,000 whites—supplied 50 per cent. of the world's uranium and 70 per cent. of its industrial diamonds. It used to be ruled directly from Brussels, so that both black and white had no franchise to speak of. There was no politics in the ordinary sense of the word, although John Gunther noted that there were 3,800 political prisoners.[1]

When an African in the Belgian Congo became westernized, he received special credentials so that he could enjoy some of the legal rights enjoyed by the Belgian whites. In effect the spirit of the Belgian system of *évolués* or *immatriculés* was the same as that of the Portuguese and French administations—namely, indefinite political domination.

The Belgian Africans resented being labelled, like commodities. An African observer from Rhodesia expressed the attitude of the Belgian *évolué* thus: '... some educated self-respecting Africans refuse to qualify as *évolués*, because they regard it as being offensive to their human dignity.'[2] Their natural tendency was to regard themselves as Africans, not as Westerners.

The Belgian policy that equated domination with service was satirized by several Africans who chaffed in this strain: 'Imagine a man saying he's going to be the head of your village to serve you. Imagine the U.S.A. descending upon Belgium and declaring "We'll dominate to serve you." Imagine Russia going to Britain and offering the Belgian domination-service proposition. It's an immoral policy that, and like all immoral things it must come to a sad ending.'

As Belgian policy denied the African full citizenship in his own country it was inevitable that it was rejected by the African nationalists, and Belgium had to take a realistic view that only full independence was the real solution to the problem. In 1960 they granted the Congo full independence and in 1962 they also granted Rwanda and Burundi full independence. Thus they granted what their

[1] John Gunther, *Inside Africa*, Hamish Hamilton Ltd., London, 1955 p. 659.
[2] *The African Parade*, February 1957, p. 22.

system of *évolués* had purported to deny the African masses—full political participation.

To think of South Africa is to think of apartheid. Apartheid is an Afrikaner word meaning apartness or separateness. As a political instrument it means social, economic, political, and sexual segregation on the basis of race. It is an effort to isolate from one another the white and the black races. But since geographical separation is not feasible, the apartheid policy becomes in practice one of both isolation and association. For practical reasons whites associate with blacks, but for the purposes of dominating the African, they isolate themselves, by law, from the Africans. Prime Minister Strijdom's slogan was *baaskap*—white supremacy. He plainly stated his case, 'The white man will only succeed in remaining in South Africa if there is discrimination, in other words, only if we retain power in our hands.'[1]

Here is the real purpose of discrimination. It is an instrument to concentrate political power in Afrikaner or European hands. Strijdom could not have stated the case more frankly. When Dr. Verwoerd took over in 1958, after Strijdom's death, he carried the spirit of *baaskap* to its logical conclusion, and his successor, Mr. Vorster, is still implementing it today (1967) in the form of Bantustans. Apartheid is an 'underdog-making' policy, and the most objectionable expression of white supremacy.

But even the Republic of South Africa, in spite of its deaf ear to the legitimate demands of African nationalism voiced through the African nationalist movements, Pan-Africanism, and the United Nations, has not remained altogether uninfluenced and unaffected. The creation of Bantustans with a bogus self-government was, from start to finish, intended to placate critical world opinion. The African nationalists have rejected Bantustans on the grounds that they are counterfeits of freedom and independence. Pressures both internal and external are building up: other oppressive and freedom-denying policies have fallen by the way, and it is not presumptuous to surmise that the apartheid policy is bound to fall too. International opinion is set against a policy of this nature. Some white people have even joined the blacks to wage a relentless war against it.

In different parts of British Africa British policy assumed various forms. After the British government had experienced strong revolts in North America its policy of close control over the colonies changed to one of granting independence. British policy in British Africa was

[1] T. W. Wallbank, op. cit., p. 86.

one of training Africans for eventual self-government within the Commonwealth of Nations. In place of an exclusive policy that created only a white government, the tendency of the British was to have a central government of the country reflecting the different races living in that country. This type of government was called multiracial. The evolution of this form of government remedied up to a point some of the glaring anomalies in British African administration.

British policy, in theory looking forward to eventual self-government of the British colonies, in practice boiled down to one of 'Hold as long as you can'. Of course, this is understandable when it is remembered that the British were not in Africa primarily for the good of Africa. They were there primarily for their own good. It is evident, therefore, that their paper policy of eventual self-government for the colonies implied self-liquidation, which was by no means an easy thing to do as this was diametrically opposed to their interests. No one liquidates himself willingly, and this is why nearly every country that eventually received full independence from Britain first experienced a period of arrests and widespread imprisonment. It is a standing joke that 'when the British start arresting, full independence is around the corner'.

British policy was, however, the best of all European policies in Africa in that it was realistic enough to accept the inevitable result that the country must eventually revert to its rightful owners. Although in many parts of British Africa the Africans were socially, economically, politically, and educationally discriminated against, nevertheless they enjoyed direct representation, even if out of proportion to their overwhelming numbers. British policy, like other European policies in Africa, subscribed to the doctrine of white supremacy, not only in theory, but also in practice.

A European policy common to all the colonial powers was gradualism. According to this policy, the African peoples were to be developed slowly, as rapid development would have the effect of upsetting the orderly process of evolution. The white man was to set the pace of this development. African progress—its volume and its rate—was to be given in small doses like prescribed medicine lest big quantities destroy the immature African. What did gradualism mean for the African in practical terms ? Socially, it meant that only a few Africans were to be treated as real human beings. Economically, it meant that the African had to be placed on a basis of deliberately depressed economy to ensure his indefinite subservience to the white man, and to ensure white domination of him. Politically, it meant holding all effective political power in white hands for the purpose of maintaining the position of white supremacy. Educationally, it meant fewer educational facilities for the African peoples. Gradualism was in substance a practical implementation of white supremacy. Historically and logically gradualism was a political device to hold back the normal rights and privileges of the African peoples.

There was another political doctrine propounded by the colonial powers, and that was the paramountcy of native interests. This first commended itself to the colonial powers and white settlers since it was assumed that it was the white man who would decide what was, and what was not, a paramount native interest. But soon the whites realized its intrinsic flaws—namely, that the claims of the 'paramountcy of native interests' coincided with those of African nationalism! The whites had no alternative but to reverse their own doctrine.

Elsewhere in European-ruled Africa the doctrine of 'trusteeship' was propounded to justify the presence of the white man. The white man according to this doctrine held Africa in trust for the African. The white man was mature and the African immature, and therefore, so it was argued, the mature should hold Africa in trust for the immature. But the white man, the exponent of this doctrine, soon discovered that this doctrine looked forward to a time when the white man would wind up business in Africa. This doctrine was a blind ally of African nationalism, and when the white man realized this he rejected it.

The doctrine of partnership in the now defunct Federation of Rhodesia and Nyasaland sired by the white-settler politicians was another practical political instrument to entrench white supremacy. When its architects were pressed for a clear definition they openly said that the partnership envisaged between black and white in Central Africa was to be the same as the one that existed between rider and horse, it being assumed that the European was the rider and the African the horse! It takes at least two to make a contract, and free consent is the only effective instrument of any partnership. But when some European liberals pointed out that the 'rider and horse' doctrine was a shocking definition which could only serve to engender hostilities between black and white, the white Central African politicians abandoned it and hammered out a new definition —'senior and junior' partners—that is, white and black were to be senior and junior partners, it being understood that the white man was to be the senior partner and the black man the junior. The 'rider and horse' theory and the 'senior-and-junior-partner' theory, though differently worded, were fundamentally one and the same thing. The common basis of both definitions was indefinite subservience of the black to the white man, and indefinite domination by the white man over the black man.

The overall European policy in Africa may be summed up in these two words—white supremacy, and this is what the African means when he says, 'White people, from Cape to Cairo, are the same.' That is, they have a mania to rule Africa. This European policy was a great challenge to Africa, and since it is the nature of human existence to respond to challenge, the African peoples, despite their great geographical, linguistic, and ethnic differences, were united by this challenge. So long as the challenge remained, the African continued to respond positively and persistently by every conceivable means to overthrow white domination.

An examination of the ingredients that make up African nationalism may be enumerated as the African's desire to participate fully in the central government of the country; his desire for economic justice that recognizes fully the principle of 'equal pay for equal work' regardless of the skin colour; his desire to have full political rights in his own country; his dislike of being treated as a stranger in the land of his birth; his dislike of being treated as a means for the white man's end; and his dislike of the laws of the country that prescribed for him a permanent position of inferiority as a human being. It was this exclusive policy of white supremacy that brought to the fore the African's 'consciousness of kind'.

Since this exclusive policy was largely responsible for the emergence of African nationalism, what European policy would have done the job better? Perhaps an inclusive one. By definition an inclusive policy takes in all those who come under its purview, and this is its chief merit since it does not ignore the needs of one section of the population in favour of the other. But white supremacy by definition is exclusive and could not therefore become inclusive. Take away exclusiveness and white supremacy dies a natural death. White supremacy had to be exterminated first to make room for an inclusive policy.

CHAPTER 14

White Supremacy in Action

In this chapter white supremacy is to be looked at in action, and not so much as an ideology. How did this doctrine affect Africans in their daily life?

The white man had not come to Africa for the sake of ruling it. He did not rule Africa for ruling's sake. He ruled Africa so that he was in a better position to exploit the natural resources of the continent. He came to Africa purely for his own good. The benefits that the white man sought in Africa were fundamentally economic. He only established white supremacy as a means to an end, and not as an end in itself. White supremacy was merely a mechanism to enable him to have the lion's share of the economic wealth of Africa.

Since white supremacy was the watchdog of white economic interests European rulers made laws that were weighted against the African peoples. The African, legally, had to be made to hold the thin end of the economic wedge, and the white man the fat end. That the African received less of everything because his standard of living was low, was just a lie in the soul.

Land is the basis of all wealth, and the white man made sure that he controlled most of the land. At one time 13·1 per cent. of the land in the Republic of South Africa belonged to Africans who formed 64 per cent. of the total population; in Rhodesia Africans occupy, but do not own, 38 per cent. of the land although they constitute 95 per cent. of the population; in Kenya the Mau Mau revolt of 1951 was the result of the land hunger created by the process of declaring European those parts of the country the white man wanted, and then removing Africans from such lands. The Europeans often gave themselves the choicest parts of the land, and the worst parts were designated as 'Native Reserves'. But this was not all: they owned most of the land in spite of their low numerical strength.

What was the effect of this unequal and inequitable distribution of land? Although the country was sparsely populated, it created population explosions in the 'Native Reserves'. This surplus population was forced out of the 'Native Reserves' on to European farms where they had no other alternative than to be employed by European farmers at the low wages which allowed the farmers super-profits. Land-hungry Africans were allowed to build their homes and till some land in return for agricultural services rendered to European farmers during the ploughing and harvesting seasons. Thus the feudal system characteristic of the Middle Ages, but which was destroyed during the fifteen and sixteenth centuries, was resurrected in Africa during the latter half of the nineteenth century and practised during most of the twentieth century. The Africans had to pander to the whims of the European farmer or else he lost his home on the European farm. If the African forced out of the 'Native Reserve' did not find a job or a home on European farms, he was forced to seek employment in the cities, towns, and mines. Hence African nationalists viewed these deliberately created population explosions, in scantily populated African countries, as an ingenious device of meeting European labour problems on the numerous European farms and in the expanding industries.

An African population was thus created which had no roots in the 'Native Reserves' or in the European farms, cities, towns, or mines. The African was placed entirely at the mercy of European employers who were only prepared to pay him the lowest possible wages. The African was deprived of any bargaining power for his services. The African was dispossessed not only of his land, but of his culture, his personality and integrity. A man whose home is built on a European property is not the same as the man whose home is built on his own property. Insecurity, anxiety, and uncertainty constantly gnaw at his very soul, disturb his tranquillity, and undermine the very basis of his manhood. Disturb the people's land, and you disturb their lives.

Another important result of crowding the African in the 'Reserves' like sardines in a tin was that this gave rise to overstocking or cattle population explosion. Overstocking became a real problem, and what did the European governments do about this? They passed laws limiting the number of cattle an African might own, and if the African refused to act in accordance with the destocking law, the law dealt with him accordingly. Of course, the European governments did all this in the name of preventing soil erosion, conserving soil and water and flora! And these measures, in actual practice, turned out to be effective instruments in preventing white supremacy from being eroded and in conserving white supremacy! The sore point among many Africans, however, was that the African people were, in effect, not allowed to keep the natural increase of their stock since it was in excess of the legally permissible number that each African was enjoined to keep. The European governments organized regular cattle sales throughout the 'Native Reserves' so as to facilitate the disposal of these cattle in excess of the required number. The regular buyers were, of course, Europeans who lived off the fat of the land.

The surplus population of the 'Native Reserves' was thus to the great disadvantage of the African peoples but to the great advantage of Europeans. Phyllis Ntantala has this to say about South Africa:

If we compare the rural land area with the rural population, we find that 124,186,000 morgen of land are owned and occupied by only 700,000 whites, while 6,025,547 Africans are crowded into 17,518,977 morgen of crown land called the 'Native Reserves'. The problem of the African, the cause behind this story of a people's agony, is LAND-LESSNESS: LANDLESSNESS, so that the people will be forced out into the labour market, to the mines and the farms where they will be herded together in camps, compounds and locations, where each white industrialist, farmer and housewife will be allotted his or her fair share of hands. In the towns only their labour is wanted—themselves not.[1]

The African's problem was twofold. Human population explosion, created by the unfair distribution of land, deprived him of his land, and the cattle population explosion, again created by unfair distribution of land, robbed him of his cattle. These exploded the very basis of his livelihood and human personality, while they were the answer to the white man's labour problems and his super-profit motive. Europeans therefore took every care to see that African economic disadvantages were legalized so that they could be effectively enforced by the police and by the courts. The courts had no alternative other than to administer the law as it was, even though it was stinking with economic injustice, and this was why African nationalists usually characterized the courts as 'rubber-stamps of injustice'. If a European farmer or industrialist ran short of labour, he just applied a little pressure on the European Member of Parliament who represented his constituency, and in turn the M.P. pressed the button in the white legislative assembly and out came cheap native labour in abundance through the other end! A government which could not provide by legislation cheap native labour was considered inefficient and ran the risk of being thrown out of power prematurely or at

[1] 'African Tragedy', *Africa South*, vol. 1, No. 3, April–June 1957, p. 67.

the next general election. 'Give me plenty of cheap native labour, and I will give you my vote,' was the bargaining strength of the European elector faced by vote-seeking parliamentary candidates. There was no African vote to counteract this 'cheap-native-labour' trend of the European voter.

So much for land and cattle. The structure of wages and salaries in European-ruled Africa should now be considered. Not only did the white man apportion to himself the choicest and most of the land, but he also saw to it that the lion's share of wages and salaries went to him. It was maintained that since the white man had the skill, the experience, and the necessary qualifications it was only fair that he receive higher wages than the African who, it was argued, had less skill, little experience, and lacked the necessary qualifications. Experience in all European-ruled Africa, however, soon proved that this was yet another lie in the soul, because when the African became as skilled, as experienced, and as qualified as the European himself the wage structure was still weighted against him: the true reason was to be found only in the unwillingness of the European to share equal wages with the African. The logic of the whole foundation and structure of white supremacy was firmly set against the sound principle of 'equal pay for equal work'. It was left to African nationalism to destroy first white supremacy in order to pave the way for those congenial conditions that would help 'equal pay for equal work' to materialize. In the distribution of salaries and wages, the spirit of that exercise may be better depicted in the following story:

A lion, a hyena, and a jackal agreed to go hunting together but only on one condition, that whatever they killed they would share equally among themselves. A big fat antelope they soon sighted, and after him they went with a swiftness that seemed to bear them on the air. The big fat antelope they soon killed, and the lion quickly presided over the distribution, while the other two looked on with enthusiasm.

Giving the hyena a portion the lion said, 'You take this,' and giving himself a similar portion he said, 'and I will take this.' Giving the jackal a similar portion he continued, 'You take this,' and giving himself another portion he said, 'and I will take this.' And so he continued the supposed equal distribution of the booty, 'You take this and I will take this. You take this and I will take this.' He repeated this round six times until the distribution was finished.

The net result of this sharing showed that the lion had received most meat, and therefore the principle of 'equal sharing' had been violated, but had been scrupulously observed between the shares that fell to the jackal and the hyena who both complained that the lion had received more than had been agreed upon.

The lion, with his mane standing up, his eyes flashing with resentment, and baring his dangerous teeth, said, 'I gave you, then myself. I gave you, then myself. I gave you, then myself. I gave you, then myself,' and he repeated the round six times. He explained himself further, 'You see I started with you first, and myself last. Then you, and myself last.' He went over this explanatory round six times in the most pious attitude of 'Others first, yourself last'.

'But you have four more pieces than both of us,' pointed out the jackal.

'These extra four pieces must be divided equally among the three of us,' insisted the hyena brightening up at the prospect of having at least one more to his share.

'Touch them if you dare,' declared the lion ready to crush any move towards his four additional shares.

The answer to the problem was not to be sought in the contract of the three gentlemen, but in the appetite or greed of the lion, and there ended the matter.

How did white supremacy work socially? In the Republic of South Africa one can still see signs in large letters such as EUROPEANS ONLY, in public parks, entrances, buses, railway stations, and other public places. During the life of the Federation of Rhodesia and Nyasaland which came into being in 1958 against the monolithic opposition of the African people, but which the African nationalists helped to destroy under the leadership of Dr. H. K. Banda, such signs were the order of the day. These signs were also to be seen in Kenya. This was only open public racial discrimination; we cannot go into other subtle and sly ways in which the African was often discriminated against.

John Gunther is impartial and an authority with an unusually keen insight into the problems confronting twentieth-century Africa. He writes:

In some respects segregation is more pronounced in the Rhodesias than anywhere else in Africa, even Kenya and the Union (South Africa) . . . racial discriminations in Rhodesia are among the most barbarous, shameful, and disgusting in the world.

In Lusaka (Northern Rhodesia) when we were there Africans were n ot allowed in most European shops, but had to use hatchways.They stood in line out in the dust or rain in dark passageways on the side of or behind the shop, where a kind of peephole with a small ledge was built into the wall. Through this hatch they called out their wants, and merchandise was (if the white man inside chose to pay attention) pushed out to them through the slot. Africans were not allowed to touch or handle articles; they could not feel the texture of a bit of cloth or try on things, and they had no opportunity for looking around or making any choice.[1]

This social discrimination did not end only in hotels and restaurants which closed their doors to African people. Cohabitation of black and white was made a criminal offence. In Rhodesia the Immorality Act (which became defunct in 1962) had been designed to this end. As a result of this social bar many a European female who was found cohabiting with her black lover had to cry 'rape' to satisfy the uncompromising demands of white supremacy, and in so doing sent her black lover, who sat so high in her heart, to the gallows! She had to murder her own lover to appease white supremacy.

In perusing the annals of courts in European-ruled Africa, I have failed to discover a single instance where a European was convicted of the murder of an African and sentenced to death, although many cases have been found of Europeans convicted of murder of Europeans and sentenced to death. Many cases of Africans convicted of murder of Europeans and Africans and sentenced to death have also been found. In other words, no white man in the whole colonial history of Africa was ever sentenced to death for the murder of an African! White supremacy viewed natives as things, and therefore in the eyes of white supremacy it was preposterous and unthinkable to take away a man's life for having killed a thing! Perhaps a diversion at this juncture is excusable, and by quoting from Arnold Toynbee as to how white people generally viewed the African people whom they called 'natives' these assertions may be clarified:

When we Westerners call people 'Natives' we implicitly take the cultural colour out of our perceptions of them. We see them as trees walking, or as wild animals infesting the country in which we happen to come across them. In fact, we see them as part of the local flora and fauna, and not as men of like passions with ourselves; and, seeing them thus as something infra-human, we feel entitled to treat them as though they did not possess ordinary human rights. They are merely natives of the lands which they occupy; and no term of occupancy can be long enough to confer any prescriptive right. Their tenure is as provisional

[1] John Gunther, op. cit., pp. 619–20.

and precarious as that of the forest trees which the Western pioneer fells or that of the big game which he shoots down. And how shall the 'civilized' Lords of Creation treat the human game, when in their own good time they come to take possession of the land which, by right of eminent domain, is indefeasibly their own? Shall they treat these 'Natives' as vermin to be exterminated, or as domesticable animals to be turned into hewers of wood and drawers of water? No other alternative need be considered, if 'niggers have no souls'. All this is implicit in the word 'Natives', as we have come to use it in the English language in our time.[1]

Perhaps in fairness to the white people, it should be pointed out that it is not only they who tend to look at other people in this fashion. It is a universal trait among all conquerors regardless of the colour of their skins, their creeds and nationalities. The conqueror attitude always tends to downgrade the humanity of the conquered, and this was why European conquest of Africa had to be liquidated altogether, and why African nationalism—that God-sent force which gathered momentum after World War II—discharged its head-waters in the 1950s and 1960s and swept away most white supremacy into the Atlantic Ocean, the Indian Ocean, and the Mediterranean Sea. No other force in Africa could have done it so effectively. It is clear from what has been said so far that white supremacy was the European rejection of the African as a full man in his own country, and African nationalism was the rejection of that doctrine. One or the other had to give way. There was to be no compromise.

[1] Arnold J. Toynbee, *A Study of History*, Oxford University Press, London, 1934, vol. 1, p. 152.

CHAPTER 15

The Majority Mind of Europeans

The European in Africa found himself surrounded by many enemies of his own making. This arose out of his unwillingness to share citizenship with people outside his racial group. The white man's determination to impose his will on Africa, regardless of what the Africans felt, created a situation in which the white man found himself surrounded by fires which could be extinguished easily if only he took the right attitude towards other people outside his own race. In a sense the white man found himself between two big fires. On the one hand he feared the march and triumph of democracy in Africa since this implied the annihilation of white supremacy to which he clung so dearly. On the other hand the white man feared the possible rise of communism in Africa since democracy and communism can never dwell under the same roof. With one hand the white man in Africa seemed to be saying, 'Keep communism out of Africa,' and with the other he seemed to be saying, 'Keep democracy away from the Africans.'

But fate seemed to have sealed the doom of white supremacy since, if either communism or democracy were established on the continent of Africa, white supremacy would be doomed. Viewed from this angle democracy and communism formed an unholy alliance which exploded white supremacy. Added to this unholy pact was African nationalism which strengthened the hands of democracy to the detriment of white supremacy. The white man feared communism since it was based on the will of the majority, and in this case the majority were the Africans whom the white man excluded from any participation in the central government of the country; he feared nationalism since it demanded the extension of democracy to the majority of the people, who happened to be non-white. It was at this point that the honest thinking of the white man in Africa broke down, fearing a reversion to the law of the jungle whereby the weakest animal is at the mercy of the strongest. It was Aneurin Bevan who warned during the Anglo-French military invasion of Egypt, 'If the government wants to reimpose the law of the jungle, they must remember that Britain and France are not the most powerful animals in it. There are much more dangerous animals prowling around.'

This ambivalence on the part of the European in Africa produced what we call a split mind, a mind that subtly and openly defied the ordinary moral laws when it came to matters that affected the freedom and independence of the African people. The European in Africa, though he claimed to be a champion of democracy, was democracy's worst enemy since he was determined to see that democracy was not extended to the millions of Africans who were actually demanding it. It seems reasonable that if democracy was reserved for Europeans, then the teeming millions of Africans had to find something else in its place. However disagreeable the memory of Mau Mau terrorism, an objective student cannot help being impressed by the fact that the whole movement was one of desperation seeking the recognition of legitimate claims of the African people. The Mau Mau members resorted to desperate measures because they wanted a say in the affairs of their country. The Mau Mau movement shook the British out of their political complacency and this, though at a terrible cost of human life, was to the good.

The French provide another good example of how European powers moved heaven and earth to see that democracy in Africa remained the white man's monopoly. The French policy towards Africans who demanded self-government was one of brutal repression. In Morocco, for instance, when the Arabs demanded their full independence, the French deposed the rightful Sultan Mohammed V and replaced him with their puppet Sultan Bew Arafa. The difference between the two Sultans was that Mohammed V resisted the imposition of the French people upon the Arabs, whereas Ben Arafa supported the French imposition. The Moroccans retaliated by massacring over 2,000 French *colons* and the French army and Air Force answered by destroying whole tribes and villages. It is believed that 6,000 Arabs were killed. All this was to fulfil the French prayer, 'The will of French people shall be done in Morocco as it is in France.' But the Moroccans were equally determined—'The will of the Moroccans, and not of the French, shall be done in Morocco.' With the return of Mohammed V to Morocco and the granting of independence to the Moroccans, peace and order returned to this part of Africa.

Algeria was the next to demand full independence from France, and the same brutal repression greeted her. It is estimated that there were in 1957 more than 300,000 French troops ready to fight the Algerian rebels. It was calculated by French military experts that if this number could be increased to 400,000, the whole Algerian revolt would be wiped out. Because the Algerians demanded full independence, they were to be wiped out, and only those who submitted to the will of the French were to be left. To many African observers the Russian brutality during the Hungarian revolt could not surpass that of France in the Algerian revolt. It is seen that an African who aspired to democracy was as much an object of European hatred and suspicion as one who tried to embrace communism. An African democrat, or communist, or nationalist, was a target for French bullets. In short, the French aimed at making the Algerians count for nothing, but the Algerians resisted this 'nothing-fiction' of the Algerian people.

It has been stated elsewhere that democracy is the 'will of the majority'. The essence of dictatorship is just the reverse—'the will of the minority'. Democracy as practised in Britain, western Europe, and the U.S.A. accords roughly with the classical definition, but democracy as practised by European powers in Africa agreed with the standard definition of dictatorship. It was much closer to dictatorship since European powers owed their existence in Africa to military force and not to the will of the majority. The people had no constitutional means of overthrowing any white government that mismanaged their affairs. Surely, for the 150,000,000 Africans to be at the mercy of 5,000,000 whites could not be said to be African or European democracy.

In dealing with one another, Europeans followed democratic methods, but in their dealings with the African they adopted dictatorial methods. Democracy for themselves, and dictatorship for Africans! This is what is meant by the European 'split mind'—a mind that pursued two radically opposite political ideologies.

In the rest of this chapter an attempt will be made to interpret the European mind with regard to the question of African freedom and independence so that the reader may see clearly what was involved in the nationalistic struggle that went on in Africa. Our line of inquiry will describe and explain the impressions made on the African mind by political pronouncements made by leading Europeans. We propose taking even the most important men and laying them on our political operation table, and conducting a thorough surgical examination, since what they said and did greatly affected the body politic of Africa.

Sir Winston Churchill once said he did not become Prime Minister of Britain in order to preside over the liquidation of His Majesty's Empire. This was said at the time India was demanding full independence from Britain. To the African that meant only one thing: that Sir Winston Churchill was determined to perpetuate British imperialism, which meant the perpetuation of African subjection. Many an African wondered how it was that the same man who opposed Nazi domination could make a statement that purported the very thing against which he had so heroically stood. It became clear that while Sir Winston Churchill had once championed the cause of Western democracy, he was unwilling to extend the same democracy to colonial peoples. To the Africans it sounded like, 'Freedom for the British, and subjection for the African'. It was this apparent double standard which baffled many an African in his attempt to understand Western peoples.

Albert Schweitzer, who did so much for thousands of African people in his lifetime, also forms a rewarding study of European attitudes towards the African people. John Gunther gives Albert Schweitzer's attitude towards the African people: 'The idea of the rights of man was formed and developed . . . when society was an organized and stable thing. . . . In a disordered society the very well-being of man himself often demands that his fundamental rights be abridged.'[1]

The impression this made on the African mind was that Schweitzer was averse to full African independence. He appeared to assume that there was never such a thing as organized and stable African society and that there was never such a thing as the rights of man in an African society. Schweitzer seemed to assume that African society was always disordered: but there could have been nothing farther from the truth. Although African society was simple and primitive, it had amazing organization and stability. The genius of European rule in Africa lay in the indirect rule which was based on the recognition of the social organization and stability of various African tribes. Indirect rule did not create a new order, but rather manipulated, exploited, and utilized to the full extent the pattern of life it found among the natives themselves. If Schweitzer meant that African society was disorganized and unstable, facts have proved the contrary.

From this erroneous assumption of a disordered society, Schweitzer advanced his argument of abridging some fundamental human rights in so far as these affected the African. To Africans, Schweitzer's reasoning seemed to run along these lines: 'African society is disordered. Full human rights can only be exercised properly in a

[1] Quoted in John Gunther, op. cit., p. 717.

well-ordered society. Therefore, since African society is disordered, African human rights must be abridged.'

This interpretation of Schweitzer may look somewhat exaggerated, but a justification for it can be attempted. The African looked around him to see the practical implications of this theory of abridging fundamental human rights, and he was more and more impressed by what he saw meted out against him by the European powers. He observed that many times when African workers went on strike the government declared a state of emergency, thus placing the African leaders at the mercy of the law. But when European strikes happened, no such emergency measures were taken. The African further noted that when African political organizations fought against discriminatory legislation, the government (which was usually white) passed laws that almost neutralized such organizations. The African noted that whenever the Africans demanded their freedom, which was their birthright, the leaders of such freedom-movements were quickly arrested, and Schweitzer's meaning of abridging fundamental human rights became very clear to the African.

What does abridging fundamental human rights mean? To abridge the fundamental rights of man is to take away some of these rights but to leave others, both the quality and quantity of which are determined by the one who chooses to abridge them. What are these human rights? Equality of human beings in dignity and rights; freedom from discrimination on the ground of race, colour, sex, language, religion, and political creeds, and freedom of speech, expression, enterprise, and the press. Freedom of self-determination of all peoples is one of these fundamental human rights.

It is clear then that to abridge any rights was to interfere with fundamental human rights. To accept this doctrine of abridging these rights was to place one group of people at the mercy of another: to abridge African human rights was to place the African people at the mercy of European powers.

If this were an acceptable doctrine, it would mean that these European powers were the chief source of the fundamental human rights of the African while actually the African derived his human rights, not from the fact that he belonged to this or that European power, but from the fact that he belonged to the human family. It is obvious, therefore, that the abridger of fundamental human rights is a dictator—the very antithesis of democracy.

Perhaps Slobodan M. Draskovich has a point which is helpful at this juncture. In his brilliant analysis of the nature of communism he observes: '. . . the right of peoples to freedom, independence and self-determination is recognized only if and when it serves the interests of the communist revolution and the consolidation of communist power.'[1] He might as well have said: 'The communists abridge fundamental human rights where their interests are threatened.'

Joseph Stalin once said:

There are occasions when the right of self-determination conflicts with . . . higher right—the right of the working class that has assumed power to consolidate its power. In such cases—this must be said bluntly—the right of self-determination cannot and must not serve as an obstacle to the exercise by the working class of its right to dictatorship. The former must give way to the latter. That, for instance, was the case in 1920, when in order to defend the power of the working class, we were obliged to march on Warsaw.

Clearly communism purports, not to deny altogether fundamental human rights, but to abridge them. Joseph Stalin stood for no more and for no less than the European powers stood for in Africa. The French imperialist might as well have said:

There are occasions when the African right of self-determination conflicts with . . . higher right—the right of the French government that has assumed power to consolidate its power. In such cases—this must be said bluntly—the African right to self-determination cannot and must not serve as an obstacle to the exercise by the French government of its right to sovereignty. The former must give way to the latter. That, for instance, was the case in 1957, when in order to defend the French rule, we were obliged to march on Algeria.

Another interesting aspect of Schweitzer's thinking is his 'elder brother' theory. He said:

A word about the relations of the whites and the blacks. What must be the general character of the intercourse between them? Am I to treat the black man as my equal or my inferior? I must show him that I can respect the dignity of human personality in everyone, and this attitude in me he must be able to see for himself; but the essential thing is that there shall be real brotherliness. How far this is to find complete expression in the sayings and the doings of daily life must be settled by circumstances. The Negro is a child, and with children nothing can be done without the use of authority. We must, therefore,

[1] S. M. Draskovich, *Tito: Moscow's Trojan Horse*, pp. 32–3.

so arrange the circumstances of daily life that my natural authority can find expression. With regard to the Negroes, then, I have coined the formula: 'I am your brother, it is true, but your elder brother.'[1]

Schweitzer (like the Dutch who regarded the Indonesians as innocent children who needed at all times Dutch paternal care) played the common role of the big white father. This reminds me of a conversation I had one day with a white student. 'You see, Sithole, we don't like Nasser,' he said.

'Why don't you?' I asked him.

'Because he is inclined more towards Russia', said he, as if inclination towards Russia and disinclination from the West merited death itself.

'Well,' said I, 'what else could he do? He wanted to buy arms from the Western powers, and he was carefully controlled as to what to buy.'

'But you see,' he said, 'selling arms to Egypt would be like selling arms to a child, and you know what happens when arms are in the hands of children.'

'That's exactly the reason why Nasser has turned to Russia. We all like to deal with those who treat us like men, not with those who treat us like little children.'

This attitude of treating all non-Westerners like children was prevalent among Westerners. The Dutch were surprised when the Indonesians, whom they had treated all along like little children, led a successful revolution which ended in the freedom and full independence of more than 78,000,000 Indonesians. The African interpretation of Schweitzer's regarding the African as a child was correct—namely, that Schweitzer deliberately reduced an adult African to a child so that he could justify the superimposition of European authority on the African.

Schweitzer admitted the fact that the black man and the white man were brothers, but he qualified this by saying that the white man was the black man's elder brother. The black man was therefore the younger brother of the white man. In African society the elder brother is looked up to by the young brother in this life and the life to come. In politics, the elder brother theory would mean domination of the Africans by whites. The African saw in this theory not temporary but permanent domination of the African people, since chronologically the younger brother never can catch up with the

[1] C. R. Joy (ed.), *Albert Schweitzer: An Anthology*, A. & C. Black Ltd., London, p. 85.

elder brother. While Schweitzer's acceptance of the concept of brotherliness between black and white commended itself to the heart of the African, yet its elder brother aspect struck deep fear into his heart. It suggested very strongly to the African that at the back of Schweitzer's mind was indefinite African subjection. His three theories—namely, abridging some of the fundamental human rights of the African, that the Negro was a child and therefore the white man was his father, and that the white man was the black man's elder brother—strongly supported the common view among the African thinkers that, fundamentally, Schweitzer was opposed to racial equality in any form. This view of Schweitzer's was, moreover, shared by many white people.

This attitude was shown in the European policy of multiracialism in European-ruled Africa. While multiracialism allowed group participation, and recognized group rights, it denied individual citizenship rights. Multiracialism as practised in British East Africa, for instance, meant that other races were allowed to participate in government affairs so long as they were satisfied with a secondary place in the whole scheme, while the first place was reserved for whites only. Multiracialism as an instrument of government was a subtle entrenchment of white supremacy, a domination of one race by another, a rule by minority and not by majority, and a refusal to create a common electorate.

The Kenya settlers put it more openly when they said: 'We are opposed to any scheme of provincial independence which might go so far as to deprive Europeans of leadership and control of the colony as a whole.'[1]

Multiracialism often puzzled the African when he tried to distinguish between dictators and European powers in Africa. The two seemed to be blood-brothers. They both sought the domination of other people. To refuse adult universal franchise was to refuse the granting of some of the basic human rights to the majority. The triumph of multiracialism if it had remained as it was would have been the triumph of white supremacy and the perpetuation of African subjection.

Cecil John Rhodes coined the dictum 'Equal rights for all civilized men' in reference to British-occupied Africa. This dictum, as it did not promise to give these rights immediately to the African, was easily accepted by Europeans because at that time there was hardly any African who opposed sufficient externals of Western

[1] *Africa South*, Vol. 1, No. 3, April–June 1957, p. 73.

civilization. But in the course of time the situation changed, and the white man, in view of the presence of large numbers of 'civilized' Africans, was confronted with honouring or dishonouring his promise. The idea of equal citizenship with the African was too abhorrent. And so the European found himself manufacturing countless ingenious definitions of 'civilized' so that he could exclude, with a semblance of legality, most eligible Africans from qualifying as registered voters. The political battle that went on in British East Africa and the Federation of Rhodesia and Nyasaland was, as already stated, one of forestalling the creation of adult universal franchise in favour of racial group participation. 'Racial discrimination', to borrow the Rev. George Gay's words, 'has no meaning apart from degradation.' While the African accepted multiracialism or partnership, he viewed this as an interim measure because both policies had a tendency to perpetuate white supremacy. Dr. Kwame Nkrumah was right when he said: 'I saw that the whole solution to this problem lay in political freedom for our people, for it is only when a people are politically free that other races can give them the respect that is due to them. It is impossible to talk of equality of races in other terms. No people without a government of their own can expect to be treated on the same level as peoples of independent sovereign states. . . . No race, no people, no nation can exist freely and be respected at home and abroad without political freedom.'[1]

Mr. Wellington Chirwa, M.P., sensing the real implications of the Federation imposed on the then Nyasaland, openly stated:

It is the duty of every African in this country to see that Federation is broken up so that Nyasaland should attain its full self-determination. As far as I am concerned, the right to rule this country belongs to the African people to whom it rightly belongs, and any attempt to entrench power in the hands of Europeans by any franchise system will inevitably fail and lead the country to great disaster and bitterness.[2]

The same question was taken up by Mr. Zuberi M. M. Mtemvu, in a long circular letter:

Sir Godfrey Huggins duped the British parliament and public with a slogan 'equal rights for all civilized men'. To us 'civilized' is less important than 'men'. The word 'civilized' has no such significance in our political vocabulary. Our slogan is 'equal rights for all men'. If our non-African neighbours think they are too superior to be thus

[1] Kwame Nkrumah, op. cit., pp. xiv–xv.
[2] *The Sunday Mail*, Salisbury, 16 June 1957, p. 2.

lumped together on an equality with their inferiors, that is their own business, not ours. . . .[1]

After the Tredgold Commission of Inquiry into the franchise laws of Southern Rhodesia, two separate classes of voters were recommended—A and B, the former being general and the latter special voters. The former were mostly Europeans who enjoy adult universal franchise and the latter mostly Africans with very limited franchise. In short, the whole aim of this set-up was to maintain the ascendency of A (Europeans) over B (Africans). This is what Mr. Enoch Dumbutshena meant when he said:

I expected the [Tredgold] Commission to reduce the means of qualifications so that as many people as possible could take part in the election of the members of parliament. The division of voters into two groups of varying status is to my humble mind racial. The special voters will be Africans and the Europeans will dominate the ordinary votes. Two classes of electors—an inevitable racial division.

If we get rid of the fear of racial domination, the fear of being one day dominated, then we shall find that nothing, in this business of democracy, is better than universal franchise.[2]

Jomo Kenyatta, the so-called brains of the Mau Mau movement, once said, 'A white man will always seek power over the black man. It is his nature.' Events in Africa have not discredited this saying.

The African sought to understand the European mind but this double standard of the white man puzzled him. Whatever political schemes the white man made as a solution for multiracial Africa the African remained suspicious and distrustful of them so long as they entrenched white supremacy, and hence African subjection.

Of course, it was then pointed out that for defence purposes it was extremely important that these weak and half-developed and un-developed African countries should be under some powerful European powers. It was felt that African countries needed Western defence, economic aid, Western skills and education, as if to say, 'Because Africa needs these things it must be European-ruled.'

As already stated, the white man had come to Africa first and fore-most for his own good. He did not rule Africa for her own good. He ruled her for his own good. His double-mindedness in his dealings with the peoples of Africa was a calculated move to keep himself in the position of effective power. When therefore the African later

---

[1] *East Africa and Rhodesia*, 4 April 1957, p. 1041.
[2] *Concord*, No. 11, June 1957, p. 15.

realized that he could not trust any European-made political schemes, he came to one conclusion: that if he was to count for something in his own country only full and sovereign independence could solve his problems, and he embraced African nationalism with a blind and consuming enthusiasm that borders on the holy.

CHAPTER 16

Counter-Methods

The defenders of white supremacy did not stand idle while African nationalism worked day and night to undermine the very basis of their political philosophy. It became incumbent upon them to retaliate as effectively as they could to neutralize this breathing monster called African nationalism which they came to identify as an evil force, but which African nationalists regarded as a divine gift. White settlers and the powers-that-were acted, so they righteously claimed with the seriousness of holy men, in the name of 'law and order', and they got the sympathy of their kith and kin in their homelands since in those countries 'law and order' meant all that civilization and culture had won over many centuries, whereas in European-ruled Africa 'law and order' meant the reversal of the human rights for millions. It is therefore important to examine the concept of 'law and order'.

First, what is law? Law is generally regarded as a rule of order or conduct established by authority which also enforces obedience to it. Some regard law as the appointed rules of a community or state for the control of its inhabitants. Burke says, 'law is beneficence acting by rule.'

Let us take 'law as a rule of order or conduct'. What authority establishes this? It must or should be properly constituted authority. Properly constituted authority should be based on a common will. Obedience to such a law based on properly constituted authority which in turn is based on a common will is indeed obedience to that common will. Burke seemed to suggest that law's central point is that it is beneficent and Sir W. Jones recognized in his 'State's collected will' the 'common will' which should promote 'good' and suppress 'evil'. In other words, the law is for the benefit of the majority of the people: otherwise it is purposeless. When law therefore promotes the highest good for the highest number, it becomes a blessing, but when it promotes the highest good for the lowest number, then it becomes the reverse.

Next, what is order? Order is a regular arrangement, a regular procedure. Order may also mean regular government, a desirable condition consequent upon conformity with law. In a sense order may be regarded as obedience to the law. It may also be regarded as law's achievement of purpose. In this sense, order is both the purpose and the effect of law. Burke says, 'Good order is the foundation of all good things.' Where there is no obedience to the law, and where obedience cannot be enforced, there cannot be good order.

Order's main aim is to benefit the people. In European-ruled Africa this 'good' could not possibly mean the 'good' for everybody. 'Good' was synonymous with white supremacy. If this 'good' be spelled out in more concrete terms, it would appear to mean political good, economic good, social good, educational good, and the like. In turn, political good meant white citizenship and effective white votes—and this meant the exclusion of the African from a common citizenship and the denial to the African of effective votes. Economic good meant high salaries and wages for Europeans and low salaries and wages for Africans. It meant that only Europeans were allowed to hold lucrative posts. Social good meant that all public amenities—public parks, post offices, hotels, restaurants, and the like—were run exclusively for the maximum benefit of the white man. Educational good meant providing the European child with universal education and better educational facilities, and, in turn, this meant the denial of these same benefits to the African child. This was the 'good' law in European-ruled Africa.

What was the evil that law in European-ruled Africa sought to suppress? 'Evil' is the very opposite of 'good'. In broad terms, evil may be anything that threatened 'good' as spelled out by white supremacy. African nationalism, for example, which was the sum total of all those forces which were utterly opposed to white supremacy—the 'good' which the law sought to promote—was logically and actually regarded as evil. It was therefore the aim of the law to suppress that evil—African nationalism. We can see that if African nationalism represented popular demands and aspirations, which it did, these were regarded as evil since they tended to introduce an upsetting element in the delicately balancing scales of white supremacy. The needs of a white minority were the good the law sought to promote, and the needs of the majority were the evil the same law sought to suppress.

If 'order' is the purpose of law, and the law is a practical expression or instrument of white supremacy, then that order must be a favourable response to the demands of white supremacy. 'Order' in European-ruled Africa would appear to have been no more and no less than that condition in which the African accepted his position of subservience to the white man, and that condition in which the white man was in a position to impose his will upon millions of the peoples of Africa. Order, in European-ruled Africa, meant that the relations between black and white were harmonious, and these relations were not ones based on the concept of equal opportunity, equal citizenship, and equal treatment, but rather on the concept of white domination of the African peoples. The purpose of the law was therefore to ensure this condition or state if white supremacy was to be realized as a political creed.

The evil genius of 'law and order' in European-ruled Africa was that on the one hand it accorded the white people in general full human rights while on the other it denied the African peoples the same rights. It was a two-standard law, a dualistic law, based on two eternally irreconcilable principles of freedom and unfreedom, of white-group democracy and black-group subservence, and of the highest good for the few and the lowest good for the many. It was duplicity masquerading in the name of 'law and order'. It was this inner contradiction, this inherent inconsistency of European-made laws which made the concept of 'law and order' so fundamentally different from the normal understanding of the same concept.

This is, it is hoped, a fair rendering of the concept 'law and order'. What did the white man mean in European-ruled Africa when he maintained that he was fighting African nationalism to maintain 'law and order'? This is a very important question which raises other questions: what was law and order in European-ruled Africa?

Certainly, it was not what it was in Europe or America, in Asia or in African Africa. It was not based on a common will expressed in a properly constituted authority. The so-called properly constituted authority was only a handful of Europeans who were self-appointed, and used gunpowder diplomacy combined with strong-arm methods, to make themselves the ultimate rulers of Africa. To Africans, therefore, law was a rule of order or conduct established by an external or foreign authority demanding the obedience of the indigenous inhabitants on pain of punishment. It was not a contract between the ruler and the ruled since consent, the hallmark of any contract, was entirely lacking. Order meant more or less the same thing—a regular arrangement of securing and maintaining African subservence to the white man and of maintaining white domination. It was 'a desirable condition consequent upon conformity to subservence laws'. As we have already said, the purpose of the law is good order, and good order means obedience to the law. If the law purposes to subject people indefinitely, obedience to it constitutes good order, and disobedience to it, by the same logic, implies a violation of good order.

What was said to be allowed by law had come to be regarded, among African people, as what subservience laws allowed! Under these circumstances therefore it is understandable how the virtue of law-abiding had come to be regarded by Africans as a weakness to be avoided. Defiance of such subservience laws came to be looked upon as virtue and self-respect! When the disciples of white supremacy were tackling African nationalism in the name of 'law and order', they were doing it, in reality, in the name of oppression and selfishness, since the basis of all law throughout the civilized world is not the subservience of millions to a few people sitting in the saddle of power with guns in their hands, but the common will expressed through properly constituted authority.

There were many methods employed by the white man to deal with African nationalists, but only a few will be singled out here. The main task of the white man was how to devise ways and means of crippling effectively African nationalism so that white supremacy remained intact. To do this he devised means from time to time whereby the African nationalist might be put out of political circulation for a very long time, if not indefinitely.

1. *Security Legislation:* In most parts of European-ruled Africa, laws were made in such a way that normal criticisms of the government, the police, the courts, and the white people in general were regarded by the powers-that-were as subversive and seditious of the so-called properly constituted authority. We shall quote from some of Rhodesia's so-called security legislation to show the general attitude of the white man towards the black man. The Preservation of Constitutional Government Act, Chapter 45, of Southern Rhodesia, for instance, says in part:

Any person who is a resident of Southern Rhodesia who, either within or outside Southern Rhodesia, organizes or sets up or helps to organize or set up, or advocates, urges or suggests the organization or setting up of, any group or body with a view to that group or body . . . coercing or attempting to coerce the Government, . . . shall be guilty of an offence and liable to imprisonment for a period not exceeding twenty years. . . . For the purpose of this section, 'coercing' means constraining, compelling or restraining by physical force, violence, boycott, civil disobedience or resistance to any law, whether such resistance is active or passive, or threats to apply or employ any of the means described in [this] paragraph.[1]

[1] The Preservation of Constitutional Government Act, Chap. 45, Section 2(a) (iii) (d) (i) (ii), p. 587.

Southern Rhodesia's The Law and Order (Maintenance) Act, Chapter 39, says the following in relation to strikes:

Any person who, without just cause or excuse the proof whereof lies on him, advises, encourages, incites, commands, aids or procures any other person engaged or employed in any essential service to do or omit to do any act which is likely to hinder or interfere with the carrying on of any essential service, shall be guilty of an offence and liable to imprisonment for a period not exceeding five years. . . . For the purposes of this section and of sections *thirty-three* and *forty-four* 'essential services' includes any hospital transport; any transport service; any service relating to the generation, supply or distribution of electricity; any service relating to the supply and distribution of water; any sewerage or sanitary service; any service relating to the production, supply, delivery or distribution of food, fuel and coal; any fire brigade; [and] coal mining.[1]

It is important to note that both Acts forbid boycotts and strikes as legitimate instruments of righting social wrongs. Passive resistance and peaceful demonstrations, as well as active resistance, are infringements against the law. The whole trend of the so-called security legislation is to force, one way or another, the African to accept the monopolistic rule of the white man. This trend is not only characteristic of Rhodesia, but was also typical of other European-ruled parts of Africa. Legislation in South Africa has virtually silenced the legitimate voice of the African people. In British, French, and Belgian Africa legislation was loaded against the African as a method of securing his subservience.

2. *The Police Force:* In a society which is not cursed with laws based on white supremacy, the duty of the police is to protect society, to detect crime, to prevent crime, and to see that crime is properly punished. The police have not the extra burden of having to look after white supremacy as still happens in European-ruled Africa. In European-ruled Africa police are the most effective instruments of white supremacy. They are its human forms, and little wonder that many African nationalists have often regarded the police as the right wing of the ruling European party. The following account of a personal experience of the author, has been the common experience of thousands of African nationalists in European-ruled Africa.

There had been widespread beating of African suspects by Rhodesia's police, and we felt that it was our duty to call this brutal treatment of the people to a halt. When I addressed a ZANU

[1] The Law and Order (Maintenance) Act, Chap. 39.

(Zimbabwe African National Union) rally at the Chako African Township, Chipinga, on 20 June 1964, I said:

So many of our people are being arrested and detained for days and weeks purely on suspicion, and some of the stories about the torture and torment and persecution that goes on told to us by some of these people are beyond belief. One would never have believed that such torment, torture, and persecution still go on in 1964. If the white people of this country could just go through the same treatment that those of our people who are arrested go through, they could not bear it. . . . If some of the police who actually torture our people were tortured just for two hours, perhaps they would be a little more sensible. . . .

A policeman arrests an African. He takes him to the Police Camp. He beats him. He kicks him about. He wants certain information from him. As long as the African doesn't give the desired information he must continue to go through this brutal and most humiliating treatment . . . so you get policemen all over the country going around abusing bullying, torturing, tormenting, and persecuting people. . . .

What's a policeman after all? He is a public servant, not the terrorizer of the public. The public is not there for the police, but rather the police are there for the public. The police cells have become institutions of torture, torment, and persecution. . . .

The whole speech had been spoken into a police microphone and it was recorded by the police tape recorder. After studying my speech the police charged me under the Law and Order Maintenance Act, which rendered liable to a £100 fine or a prison sentence of up to one year anybody engendering 'feelings of hostility' towards the police at any public gathering at which a policeman was present on duty.

I welcomed the charge since it had been our intention to expose the brutalities of the police. We lined up twenty-five people who had been actually assaulted severely by the police. We secured the co-operation of six doctors who had actually examined most of these police assault cases. The police got wind of our rather strong defence, and fearing real exposure, they withdrew the charge!

As it was one of their functions to see that African nationalists were put out of political circulation for a long time, they preferred forty-seven other charges against me arising out of my political activities. The hearing of these counts took five days. On forty-four of these charges the Crown failed to establish its case and therefore the defence counsel had no case to meet. When the defence counsel made an application for the withdrawal of the forty-four charges, the

Crown did not even attempt to oppose the application. What had happened was that most of the Crown witnesses (who numbered over twenty) had been assaulted first before they would co-operate with police, and the result of their forced confession tended to incriminate me. The police pressure fell dead when the Crown witnesses told the court that they had been assaulted by the police. At a later hearing the police lost their three remaining charges. This is not a special experience. It is a common experience of most nationalists.

Police provocation was, and still is, quite an effective method of dealing with African nationalism. A peaceful procession of African demonstrators is dispersed with tear gas. Confusion is created. Looting starts. Angry demonstrators run amok, and police open fire in the name of 'law and order'. The Sharpeville shootings of 1960 which resulted in the death of over seventy African demonstrators as a result of police opening fire on them is one of the notorious cases. In Rhodesia the police opened fire on peaceful African demonstrators and killed over 20 people in 1960. In 1965 a young African nationalist died in one of the police cells of the Salisbury police station as a result of continual police beatings during interrogation. At an inquest which was held later a verdict of death caused by assault was returned, but at a court hearing the policeman involved was acquitted.

3. *The I.D.R. Method:* This is imprisonment, detention, and restriction of African nationalists, and is still being widely used. Political imprisonment was and is still common in European-ruled Africa. In South Africa, for instance, when Robert Sobukwe had finished serving his three-year prison sentence he was banished to Robben Island. When Jomo Kenyatta had finished serving his seven-year jail sentence, he was sent into restriction. When Dr. Kwame Nkrumah agitated for the independence of the then Gold Coast, now Ghana, he was imprisoned for three years. The late Patrice Lumumba and Joseph Kasavubu were imprisoned for their political activities. Chief Luthuli was restricted to his home until his death. When the author finished serving his twelve-month jail sentence he was sent into restriction for a period of five years. Before U.D.I. (unilateral declaration of independence) in Rhodesia most leading African Rhodesian nationalists were restricted for periods varying from one to five years. After the illegal act the same nationalists were detained —that is, removed from restriction and placed in detention where armed guards looked after them. The Portuguese sent their African nationalists to detention islands. A good number they have killed.

4. *Armed Force:* This was, and still is, one of the most important

methods that the white man used and still uses in combating African nationalism. The Portuguese used it in the past and they still use it to maintain their possessions in Africa as integral parts of Portugal. The British used it in coping with the independence-demanding Mau Mau revolt in Kenya. They had also used it in 1896 and 1897 to quell the Matebele and Mashona rebellions. The French used it in Algeria to meet the threat of the rise of African nationalism. It should be made clear here that the armed forces were principally used internally to maintain the *status quo*.

5. *Dismissing African Nationalists:* One of the effective ways the white man used in his fight against African nationalism was to dismiss known African nationalists from employment. It should be remembered that the white man was the biggest employer. On the mine, on the farm, in the city, in the town, in the school, in the church, in all primary and secondary industries the white man was the employer, and there appeared to have been a gentlemen's agreement among the white employers to treat African nationalists and their supporters with hot ironing. Most known African nationalists were thrown out of work to force them to renounce African nationalism, and although on the whole they failed, in some cases they succeeded in neutralizing altogether some of the ardent African nationalists.

But in spite of all these strong counter-measures taken by the white man, African nationalism grew like a wild fire throughout the entire continent of Africa, and by the close of 1965 it had established thirty-six new independent African States. Only ten African countries still remain non-independent. And it would appear that it is now a question of time before these ten also become independent.

CHAPTER 17

The Cracked Myth

When this chapter was first written in 1957, the title was not 'The Cracked Myth', but 'The Cracking Myth'. At that time the myth was still cracking, but now the process of cracking is virtually over. Hence we could no longer talk of 'The Cracking Myth' but of 'The Cracked Myth'.

The first time he ever came into contact with the white man the African was overwhelmed, overawed, puzzled, perplexed, mystified, and dazzled. The white man's 'houses that move on the water', his 'bird that is not like other birds', 'his monster that spits fire and smoke and swallows people and spits them out alive', his ability to 'kill' a man and again raise him from the dead (anaesthesia), his big massive and impressive house that has many other houses in it, and many new things introduced by the white man, amazed the African. Motor cars, motor cycles, bicycles, gramophones, telegraphy, the telephone, glittering Western clothes, new ways of ploughing and planting, added to the African's sense of curiosity and novelty. Never before had the African seen such things. They were beyond his comprehension; they were outside the realm of his experience. He saw. He wondered. He mused. Here then the African came into contact with two-legged gods who chose to dwell among people instead of in the distant mountains. For the first time he came in contact with gods who had wives and children, and who kept dogs and cats.

These white gods were conscious of the magic spell they had cast over the Africans, and they did everything to maintain it. They demonstrated their control of the lightning by firing their guns regularly which to the ears of Africans sounded like thunder in the sky. There was hardly anything which the white man did which had no god-like aspects. The African, who never argues with his gods lest their wrath visit him, adopted the same attitude to the white man. And so the Africans submitted themselves to the rule of the white man without question. The white man became master in a house that was not his. He ordered the African right and left and the African was only too ready to please his white god. And the white man saw that it was good, and he smiled with deep satisfaction and said 'Africa, the white man's Paradise.' Any other race of human beings could have done the same thing under similar circumstances.

This is reminiscent of Captain Cook who played the role of a god when he and his crew landed on one of the Hawaiian islands. The natives, having never seen anyone like him and his crew before, and having never seen or heard a gun before, quickly fell on their faces and worshipped him thinking he was a god who had come from the sky. His crew they took for lesser gods. And so they gave him the full liberty of their temple where they enthroned him as their god. They were delighted that they, of all the peoples of the earth, had been chosen for a visit by the gods. Here was the chosen tribe of the Hawaiians. But as time went on some of the more intelligent among the natives began to doubt the 'goodness' of the new god for he had all the externals of any one among them. Sooner or later the natives were divided into two schools of thought—those who believed that Captain Cook was a genuine god, and those who took him only for a fake god. Neither side was convinced until one day one among them picked up a stone, and with a good aim, and with all his might, hurled it against god Captain Cook who felt the full impact of the stone and winced with pain, whereupon the untutored Hawaiian scientist triumphantly explained, 'He feels pain. Therefore he's not a god.' Great was the fury of the natives who had come to worship this god. Like hungry and angry hounds they fell upon their god, and thus died another pretender to the throne of the gods.

Right from the beginning relations between the Africans and the white people were strictly controlled and regulated. The white man made laws forbidding intermarriage and cohabitation between black and white so that this white magic spell might continue to work to the maximum benefit of the white man. A death penalty was attached to the violation of this law, but this was only applicable to the African male. To the African the law appeared to be quite unnecessary. 'How can a man cohabit with a goddess?' they asked innocently. 'How can a woman cohabit with a god?' they still wondered. The white male and his female both inhabited a higher world—that of gods and goddesses. The Matebele—the brave and warlike tribe that broke away from the Zulu nation—called the white people '*Omlimu abadla amabele*'—the gods that eat corn. The gods the Matebele had known never ate any food. In life these 'gods who eat corn' were feared above the gods the Matebele had known, the reason being that the white gods were near and visible and acted visibly whereas the usual gods were distant and invisible. The early relations between black and white in many parts of Africa were those of god and creature whose life was at the mercy of the god. The African feared to move on his own lest he incur the god's vengeful wrath. Deep mines were opened throughout the country. The dynamite that exploded the huge rocks confirmed the African's belief that the white man was a god. The African soon noticed that the white man 'has untold material wealth' and had the ability of creating even more. He soon associated all power, wealth, skills, cleverness, wisdom, and knowledge with the white man. While by nature the African did not like to stay too close to the quarters of the gods whose actions were so unpredictable, and whose fury was like a consuming fire, yet he was compelled to stay near these white gods who demanded his labour. The African soon noticed that all his people had been turned into a nation of servants for the white man, and in all fairness it must be stated that many of them enjoyed themselves by dwelling in the house of the lord for ever. And who would not rejoice to work for the gods to escape destruction?

But soon the African, while admitting to himself that there was a world of difference between himself and the white man, vaguely sensed much that was in common between them. The Matebele were not altogether wrong when they referred to the white people as 'gods who ate corn'. According to the Matebele philosophy anything that eats corn dies. Unconsciously the Matebele had sensed that beyond the white man was *Unkulunkulu*—the Great, Great One—*Usimakade*—the One who has always stood over against us. But how could they reconcile this theological belief with the wonders of the white man? The instinct of self-preservation that inclined towards treating the white man like a god triumphed temporarily over strong theological doubts.

There was a time when the white skin seemed to be all that mattered because it was mistaken for power and success in the world. There was a time when African people thought that perhaps if they had a European name that would guarantee to them success in life. African Christian converts took Western names. How could they possibly be genuine Christians without some Bible name? How could they possibly get along with the white man if all their names were African? African pastors and evangelists demanded that every African convert have a Bible name. The essence of genuine Christianity was supposed to be rather in the Bible name than in the heart of the individual. Some Africans Europeanized their African names, and so African 'Jubulani Tendele Sibanda' became 'John Philip Brown'. In some areas the process of taking on European names is still in vogue, though the motive has changed.

The psychology of all this was to identify themselves with the conqueror—to enlist the sympathy of the gods. To have no European name became a thing to be ashamed of, a kind of social stigma, a symbol of backwardness. A European name seemed to open up to the African all sorts of fantastic worlds. Anything that had anything to do with the white man had something bordering on magic. Black heroes were pushed into the background so that for some time every hero was white, and every white man was a hero. The black man became the villain in the theatre of life. So for a time the white man held the stage while his spellbound African spectators just gazed and gazed, and wondered about this new creature to whom God seemed to have given all the blessings of life.

Time is a great doctor. It heals many things. It clarifies many things. It reveals many things. Winter cannot boast that it holds sway over the entire universe all the time for sooner or later summer discredits the claim. The white man could not play the part of a god indefinitely. He could remain a myth, a mystery, for only a limited time. The myth was bound to show cracks here and there as Time rolled on to Eternity. And soon the African discovered that the white man, after all, was God-created. He had not created himself.

The African observed rather curiously that his own domestic life closely resembled that of the white man. When the African saw that the white female became pregnant like his own wife, that both the white male and white female fought, that sometimes white males fought over a white female, that sometimes an angry-with-wife white male refused to eat when he was offered food by his wife, that both the white male and white female wrinkled and stooped with age, that white people also died, he was reminded of the experiences he had in his own domestic life, and gradually he began to see through the myth.

This revelation did not stop only at the white man's domestic side of life. It extended to the African's domestic side of life as well. The white male, for some reason or other, became intensely interested in African women. When an African found a white male in the arms of an African female, he was horrified to the core of his being, for woe unto the eyes that saw the gods take such liberties. The African who had seen this god-human spectacle made sure that such an experience remained a sealed book. He feared to arouse the anger of the gods who would not only punish his iniquities but would also visit these on the members of his community. As more and more of these white males were found relaxing in the very congenial society of African ladies, the news began to be proclaimed from hilltop to hilltop in sheer amusement. The African males warned, 'Take care of our women. The gods have partaken of the forbidden fruit of Africa and may forget their own women.' The African began to resent the white man's liberties with the African female, for many an African male was sent to the gallows for cohabiting with white females. Thus on the domestic level the white man and his female were stripped of their 'god' aspects, and stood naked before the African like ordinary human beings. 'They were deceiving us,' said the African. 'We are the same.'

The narrow-minded African blamed the white man for interfering with his women, but the broad-minded rejoiced, partly because this gave a lie to the common statement that whites and blacks were basically different, and partly because they were pleased to see that despite the fact that the white man boasted of two thousand years of civilization and culture behind him, he succumbed to the charms of the African madonna. White governors, M.P.s, medical doctors, lawyers, top businessmen, postmasters, ministers of religion, and other top executives, to say nothing of the lower classes, all capitulated. This is not to deny the fact that African males fell down at the feet of white madonnas, and forgot all about their black ones. This should not surprise us because both the African male and the white male have the same thing in common, and that is the 'male principle'. Conversely the female principle seeks satisfaction in the male principle also regardless of colour or race.

There was a time in Africa when the white male's actions towards African women were said to arise from the fact that there were very few white females in Africa, but although their number increased to be equal to that of their men, the white male continued to roam the African female world. The white myth which had so overwhelmed the African could not remain the same after a white male had slept with an African female, and after an African had slept with a white female. Some white racialists tried to restrict race relations between males and females, but once the forbidden fruit had been tasted withdrawal was impossible.

There was a time when all teachers, ministers of religion, prime ministers, lawyers, judges, magistrates, medical doctors, journalists, men of letters, clerks, policemen, train, crane, and tractor drivers, postmasters, retail and wholesale merchants, and the like, were exclusively white. It was during this time that the black man used to condemn God for creating him black—for blackness had become, for him, synonymous with inability, foolishness, and backwardness. It was at this time that the African began to question whether or not the clay that went to make his body was the same as that which went to make the body of the white man. When Dr. Aggrey of the Gold Coast (now Ghana) said, 'A man who is not proud of his colour is not fit to live,' he was trying to correct this self-depreciating, apologetic attitude of many Africans. As long as all important positions remained exclusively white, the myth held together and cast its magic spell over the African. But when an army of black teachers, ministers of religion, prime ministers, lawyers, judges, magistrates, medical doctors, journalists, men of letters, clerks, policemen, train, crane, and tractor drivers, postmasters, retail and wholesale merchants, and the like made their appearance on the African scene, the white myth began to show more cracks. With the emergence now of thirty-eight fully independent African states enjoying full sovereignty, the myth which had swayed the entire continent of Africa cracked apart and was dashed to pieces beyond repair.

About twenty-four years ago, a white friend of mine in Rhodesia used to say to me, 'Sithole, it pays for a black man to get highly educated, but it does not pay the same dividends for a white man.' My friend was quite confident that a white skin, at least in Rhodesia, was enough to ensure the white man success. But events throughout Africa have belied him since now African presidents, African prime ministers, African military commanders-in-chief, African judges and African attorney-generals, and a host of others bestride the African stage. Events have cracked the white myth.

World Wars I and II also helped to widen the cracks of the white myth. Thousands of African soldiers went abroad on active service. The English street girls of London, the French street girls of Paris, and the Italian street girls of Naples did not help to preserve the white myth. Drinking and woman-raping white soldiers still added their contribution to its annihilation. White commanders ordered African soldiers to kill white enemy soldiers. African soldiers from Southern and Northern Rhodesia, Nyasaland, Tanganyika, Kenya, North Africa, French West Africa, French Equatorial Africa, the Gold Coast, and Nigeria, found themselves at the front-line war with one purpose in view—to kill every white soldier enemy they could get hold of. Many German and Italian soldiers were shot by African soldiers.

African soldiers saw white soldiers wounded, dying, and dead. Bullets had the same effect on black and white. This had a very powerful psychological impact on the African. He saw what he used to call his betters suffer defeat (though not conquest) at the hands of Germans and Japanese, and once more he was impressed by the fact that it was not the fact of being black or white that mattered. After suffering side by side with his white fellow soldiers the African never again regarded them in the same light. After spending four years hunting the white enemy soldiers the African never regarded them again as gods.

But what has this to do with the problem of the rise of African nationalism? African nationalism, in many ways, represented the degree to which the white man's magic spell had worn off. As long as this myth was thick and impenetrable the African adjusted himself as well as he could to what he thought were gods, though gods that ate corn. But the externals had had their day and reality had taken its place, though few white people in Africa realized this extremely important change.

There were certain basic facts that these white people who wanted to be regarded by Africans as myth forgot. The generations of Africans who first came into contact with the white man and his wonders were overwhelmed by the sheer novelty of the white man and the new things he had brought to Africa. But numbers of the later generation, born in modern hospitals, raised in modern towns and cities, educated in modern schools, travelling by land, air, and sea, trained in modern arts and skills, employed in modern factories and mines, rubbing shoulders daily with white people in towns, cities, schools, and on the battlefield, took the white man as a matter of course, just as they took another African. The white man could no longer cast his spell over them by a simple trick of showing them the train, or an automobile, or reading them a story book or cracking his gun because many an African then knew how to do these things. It pained the white man to realize that the African was regarding him as an ordinary human being. To him the new African generation was all degenerate. It had no proper respect for the white man, not so much because he was human, but because he was white. The white man failed to draw a distinction between what had been and what then was, let alone what had to be in a matter of a few decades.

How African was the African of that time? There was a world of difference between the African before the coming of the white man and the African afterwards. The interaction between the West and

Africa was producing a new brand of African. That is, it was pushing the white-man-worshipping African into the background, and bringing into the foreground the African who did not worship the white man. The proud and arrogant African might have thought he was 100 per cent. African because both his mother and father were African, just as the proud and arrogant white man born in Africa might have thought he was 100 per cent. European. The truth was that there was no such thing in this Africa as 100 per cent. this or that race.

Take an African who had been to school. He might have thought that he was 100 per cent. African. Physically this might have been true, but an examination of the content of his consciousness even on a superficial level, disclosed that his mathematical thought, his legal training, his theological views, his commercial and industrial undertakings, his economic theories, the themes of his conversation, his aspirations and hopes, to quote only a few, were radically different from those of an African who lived before the advent of European powers. The African of the post-European period had new eyes, as it were. He saw new things that he never saw before European rule came. He had new ears. He heard new things that he never heard before European rule came. He had come to possess a new sensibility. He felt things that he never felt before. He did not quite see what his forefathers saw. He did not quite hear what his forefathers had heard. He did not quite feel what his forefathers had felt. He ceased to see the white myth which his forefathers had seen, for the simple reason that he had ceased in many ways to be the African that his forefathers used to be.

But in what way was this African different from his forefathers? The answer is simple: his forefathers were vaguely conscious of the country in which they lived. They were not conscious of the rest of Africa—certainly not of the countries outside Africa. They spent most of their time looking after their livestock, hunting, and trapping game. Their eyes never saw the large cities and towns whose buildings now soar to the sky. They never travelled on bicycles, motor-cars, trains, and they never flew. They never went to school. That is, they never learned how to read and write. They never built themselves modern houses and schools.

The African of the post-European period lived in an environment that in many instances was different from that in which his forefathers lived. He was not only conscious of the country in which he lived, but also of Africa as a whole and of the world. Unlike his forefathers' environment that hummed with bees, that was enlivened with singing birds, disturbed by wild animals, and moved at nature's pace, the African of the European period lived in an environment where the mechanical bird had superseded the bird, where automobiles, trains, and tractors had pushed the ox, the donkey, and the horse into the background. If the African forefathers had come back to life and beheld their own descendants on the modern scene, they would have mistaken their own children for gods.

Time had given birth to a new African who was more self-assertive, more enterprising, more aggressive and more self-reliant than his forebears. It was impossible to push this new African back into time's womb just as the baby, once expelled from its mother's womb, cannot begin a successful 'back-to-the-womb' movement. The baby has to cope as well as it can with out-of-the-womb conditions. The African himself tried to cope as well as he could with the new times into which he had been born. Anyone who advised him to behave as his forefathers had behaved towards white people might as well have advised him to return into his mother's womb. Most thinking white people accepted this important change, and met the situation as it was without wasting time and effort in wishful thinking. But the attitude of the average white man was like that of dethroned gods. Their paradise has passed away with the decisive victories of African nationalism.

The now cracked myth of the white man reminds us of an incident in Shakespeare's *The Tempest*, when Caliban mistook the newcomers to his island for gods, and immediately pledged his loyalty to them. In his own words we can see the psychological impact Stephano and his friends made on Caliban during their first encounter with him.

These be fine things an if they be not sprites.
That's a brave god and bears celestial liquor:
I will kneel to him. . . .
I will swear, upon that bottle, to be thy true subject; for the liquor is not earthly. . . .
I'll show thee every fertile inch o' the island; and I will kiss thy foot: I prithee, be my god.[1]

Caliban had been thoroughly impressed that Stephano, the drunken butler, was a god from heaven, but after Time had taken its course to reveal the true nature of his new god, Caliban makes his confession:

[1] The Tempest, II, ii.

> ... and I'll be wise hereafter,
> And seek for grace. What a thrice-double ass
> Was I, to take this drunkard for a god,
> And worship this dull fool![1]

One might compare the early relations between black and white to that between child and parent. So long as the child is dependent upon the parent, the parents easily secure his loyalty and obedience, and so long as the child remains child, there is always something mythical about parents. When my wife was ten, she used to think her mother a wonderful woman because she had brought her four brothers and two sisters into the world; when her mother told her that one day she would also bring into the world babies, she used to say, 'No, impossible. I am not like you.' Her mother was a mystery to her. As long as she was ignorant of the facts of childbirth, the myth about her mother held together, but as soon as she knew these facts, the mystery fell asunder and shattered altogether, never to be reconstructed.

As soon as the African knew how to read and write, how to drive and repair an automobile, how to build a modern house and install modern plumbing, how to operate properly on a human body, how to run a business, how to do countless other things that his white god did, why, the myth fell asunder, never to come together again.

But apart from the forces described in this chapter there are other forces which contributed to the de-mythification of the white man in Africa. The presence of the independent sovereign African states has had an important role to play in this whole process. There was a time when it looked as though the natural ruler of Africa was not the African, but the white man. History, however, has reversed this, and now it is accepted that the African is the natural ruler of Africa.

From what has been said above it is clear that African nationalism was preceded by a tremendous psychological process which resulted in the de-mythification of the white man, and this psychological process was a precondition of African nationalism if the latter was to emerge and be effective. A process of internal emancipation had to precede that of political liberation.

[1] The Tempest, V, i.

PART FOUR

Nationalism's Problems

CHAPTER 18

The One/Two-Party System

'Is Africa suited to a one-party or two-party system?' Those who live in Africa and those who live outside it have asked this question again and again in their search for solutions to the many problems facing Africa today. Sometimes the question is put this way: 'Is the one-party system or the two-party system suited to Africa?'

It will be noticed that the two questions are not the same. Let us take the first one: 'Is Africa suited to a one-party or two-party system?' The assumption here seems to be that Africa should be manipulated to fit into one of these two systems. The question seems to preclude any idea that Africa is more important that either of the systems: the primary interest seems to be in the system and not in Africa!

In the question 'Is the one-party system or the two-party system suited to Africa?' the assumption is that Africa is more important than either of the systems. The question presupposes that these systems can be so manipulated as to serve Africa, not Africa to serve them. Is Africa to be the servant of these systems? Or, are these systems to be the servant of Africa?

There are many African thinkers and politicians who ardently advocate the one-party system for Africa. They are utterly opposed to the two-party system. One of the reasons advanced is that Africa has not had any two-party system in the past: the two-party system is foreign, only the one-party system is indigenous to Africa. So far as our knowledge of African political institutions in the pre-colonial era goes, no evidence of the existence of the one-party system has been found anywhere in Africa: on the contrary, the one-party system is as alien to Africa as the two-party system. If African political institutions of the past tell us anything at all, it is that if there was any system in the nature of a political party, it was a no-party system! This is historically true.

Another argument advanced in favour of the one-party system is that it enables a new government to eliminate any serious opposition so that it can devote more time and energy to the reconstruction of the new nation. Advocates of the one-party system maintain that too often the ousted colonial power stages a come-back through the opposition. Hence the elimination of the opposition is supposed to prevent neo-colonialism. Some maintain that an opposition too often cannot distinguish between party and national matters, and that this has tended to undermine the stability of the new nation.

These arguments have not been borne out by what has happened in some parts of Africa. First, the elimination of the opposition has not been the panacea for the many ills of independent Africa: in fact, the elimination of the official opposition has not eliminated the real opposition! Ghana, for instance, was legally a one-party state. On 24 February 1966 General Joseph Arthur Ankrah carried out a successful army revolt against 'Life President' Dr. Kwame Nkrumah in spite of the fact that, legally, all opposition had been silenced! On 4 January 1966 Col. Sangoule Lamizane ousted President Maurice Yameogo of the Upper Volta, in spite of the suppression of the opposition in favour of a one-party system.

On 1 January 1966 Col. Jean-Bedel Bokassa deposed President David Dacko of the Central African Republic in spite of the suppression of the opposition. In December 1965 Col. Christophe Soglo took over the Government of Dahomey in a successful military coup. In June 1965 Col. Houari Boumedienne ousted Ben Bella from the Algerian Presidency in a bloodless coup in spite of the fact that Algeria was a one-party state and all official opposition proscribed. Congo (Brazzaville) was voluntarily a one-party state before the coup which drove President Youlou out of power. In December 1963 there was an army mutiny in one-party Tanganyika (now Tanzania) which forced President Julius Nyerere to call for British military intervention which succeeded in quelling the mutiny. In Malawi, which is a one-party state in practice, there was a near revolt in 1964, but Dr. H. K. Banda acted swiftly and restored things to normal. In the one-party state of Uganda there was also a near army revolt in December 1963.

This is sufficient to show that the argument that official opposition must be eliminated in the interest of national reconstruction and stability has not been proved by historical facts. That the ousted colonial power usually stages a comeback via the opposition has also been disproved. There are other ways, and effective ones too, of staging a come-back by a former colonial power if it so wishes. The elimination of all official opposition has not prevented neo-colonialism.

After what has been said in the preceding paragraphs, it might appear that the solution is to be found in the two-party system. Those who support the two-party system say that the presence of an official opposition tends to cause the ruling party to run the country more efficiently than when there is no opposition. Justice is more easily secured for the ordinary man when there is an opposition. In other words, the ruling party has to administer real justice to prevent the opposition from coming into power and this accrues to the maximum benefit of the country as a whole. Have these arguments been borne out by facts?

There is a two-party system in the Republic of South Africa. Has this system guaranteed democracy in that country? Has it guaranteed the civil liberties of the majority of the people there? The answer is in the negative. The 12,000,000 non-European peoples there are constitutionally not citizens of the Republic of South Africa. Only the 3,000,000 Europeans there are citizens. In spite of the existence of an official opposition the majority of the people have no vote. They have been squeezed into 13 per cent. of the land while 87 per cent. of the land is at the disposal of the white minority. In Rhodesia, there is a two-party system. The constitution there provides that 23 per cent. of the seats in the Legislative Assembly are held by Africans who form 95 per cent. of the population, and 77 per cent. of the seats are held by Europeans who form only 5 per cent. of the population. In other words, the two-party system in both the Republic of South Africa and in Rhodesia has not prevented the denial of the vote to the majority of the people. The two-party system has not established political, economic, and social justice in either the Republic of South Africa or Rhodesia. The existence of official oppositions has not caused the ruling parties there to dish out justice to the majority of people in those countries.

How has the two-party system worked out in free and independent Africa?

Nigeria was a two-party state until 15 January 1966 when General Johnson Aguiyi Ironsi emerged the leader after a successful military coup. Opposition, it is important to note, was officially allowed. There was no official suppression of the opposition. In Congo (Kinshasa) where a multi-party system has existed since 1960, General Joseph Mobutu successfully ousted President Joseph Kasavubu in November 1965. There was no official suppression of the opposition, but a successful military coup, none the less, did take place there.

It might be added here that on 11 November 1965 the white Rhodesian Government, after declaring a state of emergency throughout the country and after locking up all African nationalists in prison and detention, declared Rhodesia independent from Britain. This government set Rhodesia up as a sovereign state which was not recognized by any other country, although the Republic of South Africa and Portugal were prepared to co-operate with the rebel state of Rhodesia as much as they could without openly antagonizing international opinion. They carefully observed the letter of international law, but violated its spirit!

But, of course, there are two-party states which have not had any military coups or revolutions. Zambia, which became independent in 1964, has had a two-party system since that date. The official opposition is recognized. The Somali Republic is another good case in point. The two-party system there has worked out fairly well since independence in 1960. Official opposition is allowed by the law of the land. Morocco has had a two-party system since it became independent in 1956, although it has had a near revolt once during this period of its independence.

In both one-party and two-party African states, therefore, there have been military coups or revolutions and near revolts; and there has also been national stability in these two kinds of states. The one-party system does not appear to have had any distinct advantage over the two-party-system; nor does the two-party system appear to have had any distinct advantage over the one-party system. Each system has proved both successful and unsuccessful in various parts of Africa. National success or failure cannot be sought in this or that system, but outside the system.

A party system as such is neither good nor bad just as all things are neither good nor bad. It all depends upon the use to which they are put. What is a good political system?

A good political system is one that yields maximum political satisfaction. But until it is known what 'maximum political satisfaction' any given political system is supposed to give, it is an idle academic exercise to pose the question of which system is good for independent Africa. 'Maximum political satisfaction' may mean many things and anything, and this can only be spelled out by each independent country in the light of life situations that face it. An examination of either the one-party system or the two-party system will show that each system means a different thing in each country. The one-party state of Tanzania, for instance, is quite different from that of the one-party United Arab Republic. The one-party state of Ghana was quite a different thing from that of either Kenya or Malawi. The two-party state of Nigeria was quite different from the two-party Somali Republic or the multi-party state of Congo

(Kinshasa). Even in the West, the two-party state of Great Britain is not exactly the same thing as the two-party state of the United States of America. In Europe the multi-party systems of France, Italy, West Germany, Belgium, Holland, Denmark, and the Scandinavian countries differ in many respects, although they all seem to result in the formation of coalition governments.

It is self-evident that even in this exercise of defining the concept 'maximum political satisfaction' not all African countries will see eye to eye. Each free and independent African country must define for itself this concept. This does not imply an anti-Pan-African attitude. It merely means each African country must be realistic enough and take into full account what its needs are and how best these needs can be met. Each country must sing its own tune if it is to realize itself. Other countries will accord it the respect it deserves and seek its co-operation and its friendship on the basis of its own internal strength and stability. No independent country should dance to the tune of another country—African or non-African. This is another way of saying that each African country must define 'maximum political satisfaction' for itself using the experience and the resources at its disposal.

Some political architects have suggested that the old traditional system is perhaps the best for Africa. In this traditional system the centre of power was the chief, whose office became hereditary. Perhaps the practice of life presidency in some African states is a hangover of this practice. Is rule by chieftainships feasible in modern Africa? First, we must point out that the idea of a 'political party' common to all free and independent African states cuts across the very idea of African traditional rule since elections were unknown in the modern sense, and since the leaders in the present African states may be elected from the common people, whereas under the traditional system the leaders were drawn from the royal houses and houses on which the royal houses cast their lustre. Practically all the present African political leaders came to power, not under the traditional system, but under the modern political system. African leaders cannot discard the present political system without discarding themselves. In any case, what is this African traditional system? In my view the traditional system merely represents a lower level of political evolution, and I do not accept the view that traditional rule would provide the answer to the many problems facing Africa today. I hold the view that traditionalism cannot stand the impact of modern political, social, and economic development all of which are imbued through and through with the belief that it is merit or efficiency that must count: royalty in its traditional form does not seem to mix well with the highly technological tempo of our time.

What fundamental principle must be strictly adhered to in order to achieve the satisfaction that has been carefully spelled out? Would the principle of authoritarianism help effectively to achieve this satisfaction? Or is the principle of democracy to be preferred to that of authoritarianism? Or would a mixture of both principles be more effective in achieving satisfaction? The questions of totalitarianism or dictatorship, democracy, aristocracy, plutocracy, and the like are problems to be settled by the political architects of each country.

What satisfaction is authoritarianism supposed to achieve? Is it the personal glory of the rulers, or is it the solution of popular problems? Is the rule to be personal or impersonal? If it is to be personal, what chances are there for national continuity after the personal ruler has gone? Does totalitarianism contribute to maximum national stability? Does it ensure national continuity from generation to generation?

If democracy is supposed to achieve satisfaction does this mean that this is for those in power and only the well-to-do? Does satisfaction achieved under democracy also include the masses? Under democracy, are the common people at the mercy of a wealthy few who control the instruments of government directly and indirectly? Once we settle on the principle of democracy we must then decide whether the one-party or the two-party system would be a suitable vehicle of democracy, bearing in mind that any other system outside these two could also be effective instruments of democracy.

Neither democracy nor dictatorship come into being accidentally. They come into being as a result of certain historical circumstances. If people fail to solve through democracy the problems that face them they readily resort to and accept dictatorship. If they fail to satisfy their needs through dictatorship they tend to agitate for the overthrow of the totalitarian régime in favour of democracy. It would appear that one system tends to slide into the other depending on various circumstances. This means that people adopt this or that principle—in this case democracy or dictatorship—on the basis of utilitarian considerations. What is the kernel of the matter is the problem of designing a system which achieves the maximum benefit for the maximum number, rather than a system which achieves the highest good for only a few. Politically, economically, and socially the problem is the same.

CHAPTER 19

The Desirable System

What is important therefore, is not this or that system, but what contributes to the maximum benefit for the maximum number. Anything that tends to deny the highest good to the highest number cannot solve the real problem facing free and independent Africa. All African political thinking and planning has to concentrate on this problem. Law and order is not enough; even in a slave or concentration camp there can be law and order! This satisfaction, or this good, has to be sought even beyond law and order which only touch people externally, but not internally.

The 'highest good' or the 'highest satisfaction' cannot be properly understood apart from man himself. What is our view of man? Do we believe that man was created to be a slave to his fellow man, to those who rule him, and to spend all his life as a conscious or unconscious instrument of those who happen to wield power? If our view is that people have no will of their own except that of their rulers; if our view is that people have no individuality and personality of their own except that of their own rulers; if our view is that there is no such thing as human dignity except that of the rulers; if our view is that man is not an end in himself but a means, at the disposal of his rulers, to an end; and if our view is that the people are not the centre of things but their own rulers are the centre of gravity, then the principle to adopt and to help this view is authoritarianism or totalitarianism. Normally, people like to be regarded as people and not as things; they like to think and to express what they think; they like to criticize things and persons; they see things differently and they react differently. They want to count for something. They want to feel that they can control and influence one way or another the affairs of their own country. In short, they want to be free or to feel free. Can totalitarianism satisfy these basic needs of man? Can it be maintained without enormous physical force being applied from time to time so that the totalitarian structure can hold together for the satisfaction of the rulers?

If on the other hand, our view is that man is an end in himself, and not a means to an end; if we hold that man is fully entitled to his own thinking and to the free expression of that thinking; if we maintain that man is entitled to criticize fairly things and persons around him and those in power; if we believe that self-expression of individuality and personality is basic to man's happiness; and if we adhere to the view that man has certain inherent and inalienable rights, then we cannot accept the principle of authoritarianism. We have no alternative but to settle on the principle of democracy.

Either democracy or authoritarianism can be fitted into a two-party, or one-party, or multi-party system. In Nazi Germany, for instance, totalitarianism emerged under the very nose of democracy when the latter did not seem to have any answer to the countless problems that were facing the people after War War I. People had become tired and resigned. A deep sense of insecurity ran deep, and the many political parties in Germany made many promises to right the deteriorating situation, but they never actually solved it. When Adolf Hitler appeared on the scene people supported him hoping that he would solve their many problems. It was their fervent hope that Hitler would end their frustrations, and hence they submitted themselves to dictatorship as a means of solving their pressing problems. The incompetence of the German Republic was in most respects the father of Nazi dictatorship and Adolf Hitler its midwife. If the heart of democracy is the will of the people, how are we then to call dictatorship that which has more or less popular acclamation? Is dictatorship of this nature not also based upon the will of the people? If popular will is the basis of democracy the origin of dictatorship may also be found in popular will, so democracy may differ from dictatorship only in practice but not in origin. The one-party system can be quite as an effective vehicle of either democracy or dictatorship just as the two-party system is equally capable of being used as an instrument of either democracy or dictatorship.

1. The first requirement of an ideal system that would yield maximum satisfaction or good for the maximum number is that the system shall be people-centred in a fundamental way. It must not be ruler-centred. Rulers come and go but the people as a group remain constant. This principle is extremely important since once it is admitted all other principles that make for national stability and progress become easy to accept. The one-party or two-party system can only be acceptable if it is based on this principle and rejected if it is based on the opposite principle of ruler-centredness. This is extremely important if any system is to serve a useful purpose.

The political system must serve the political needs of the people just as a child-centred type of educational system must serve the needs of the children. A politically people-centred system by definition seeks to give the highest political good to the highest number. This means that the political theoreticians of Africa must spell out these political needs. Politically, what do people need ?

(a) Man, it has been said time and again, is a political animal, and he shows this by demanding that he has a say in the running and general administration of his country. He does not want to feel that he is just a thing or a cog in the political wheel that turns round and round the affairs of his country, and with which his own welfare and his destiny are tied up. He wants to control that wheel since it affects his own life in a very real way. If he is denied this, history has shown throughout all the ages that man has worked relentlessly for the overthrow of such a system—the system that denies him a say in his own country. African nationalism, for instance, worked persistently to overthrow *eurocracy* that denied the African people a say in their own country.

(b) Free elections are one of the surest ways of assuring man that he has a say in the affairs of his own country. Free elections are people-centred in that they exercise a real influence on those who rule by election rather than by imposition. Even if those who are freely elected finally turn out to be tyrants, none the less it would be popularly elected tyranny rather than an imposed tyranny. A popularly elected tyranny is much to be preferred to an imposed one since it can be removed by vote at the next free elections, whereas an imposed tyranny can only be removed by revolutions, military coups, or other social upheavals. In any case people are much happier when they choose their own dictators than when their dictators are imposed on them. There is such a thing as a democratically elected dictator: Adolf Hitler is a good example. But of course it should be remembered that once people have elected their dictator they should also know that they cannot vote him out of power at the next free elections since it is the nature of all dictators not to allow themselves to be put out of power by those who do not control or have the military power. Where a dictator can be put out of power by the sheer casting of a vote, that system could not be called authoritarian, but democratic.

Free elections reflect the popular expression of 'the will of the people'. Both the ruling party and the opposition reflect the popular will within a given country, if that country has a two-party system. In a one-party system, the popular will can also be registered as effectively as in a two-party system. Not only do free elections reflect popular will, thereby maintaining the principle of people-centred-ness, but they also serve another useful function, and that is, they control the actions of those in power. Those in power can only remain in power by dancing to the tune of the electors who are the people. Dictators, since they do not operate under a people-centred system, do not have to dance to the tune of their electors. Rulers who ascend to power by free election are compelled by the very nature of their election to take into account the needs of those who elect them and whom they represent so that in the next elections they can still be returned to power. This may not work out perfectly but it is an effective system in the necessary interplay or interaction between the ruler and the ruled. Power being what it is (it tends to be mischievous unless controlled), it is a good thing that free elections help to keep those in power under proper control.

(c) Another principle which would ensure that any given system was based on the principle of people-centredness is the principle of free discussions. Political life, like all life, is not static. Because it changes so fast it affects the life of the people in a very real way. People need to discuss their political problems freely. New laws are made from time to time, and these laws affect the lives of the people in many ways, and therefore the people should have the full right to discuss freely these problems. We cannot accept people-centredness and at the same time reject the principle of free discussions without destroying the principle of people-centredness. It is not enough to have free elections; people must also be allowed free discussions if the principle of people-centredness is to be maintained.

(d) Another principle which should be adhered to in order to maintain the principle of people-centredness is that of free criticism. People must have the right to pass judgment on what is going on in their own country. Any system therefore which would deny the people the right of free criticism cannot be said to accommodate the principle of people-centredness.

Free criticism has a useful function in the life of any nation. First, it helps to point out what popular grievances are, and also what people need and expect of their government. This helps those in power to manage the affairs of the country much better than they would otherwise be able to do in the absence of such criticisms. Secondly, those in power cannot be aware of everything going on in the country. Some things of which they are not aware have to be brought to their attention time and again, and free criticism is one of the effective ways of doing this. If politics' chief business is the satisfaction of the feeling of the people or the effective manipulation of that feeling then that feeling must have free expression so that its real dimensions can be correctly assessed and the business of satisfying it made easier. It has been pointed out that sometimes self-expression and free criticism lead to self-explosion. Whatever this means, it is clear that the explosion in a country that allows free criticism is not as dangerous and disastrous as the explosion in a country where free criticism is not countenanced. Free criticism tends to dilute and neutralize and even prevent dangerous explosions whereas the denial of free criticism tends to ferment highly concentrated explosions which are no good for either the ruled or the ruler.

What is popularly called 'the will of the people', in a democracy, turns out, upon examination, to be 'the will of some people'. In a democracy who are the people? The people are those who can and do vote. In a 'democratic' country where the voting qualifications are so high that the majority of the people cannot vote, the people are those few who actually vote. If therefore the so-called 'will of the people', which in fact is 'the will of some people', is to be true to type, 'one man one vote' would give the claim more substance. It is illogical as well as hypocritical to advocate 'the will of the people' and at the same time deny the 'one man one vote' principle. To maintain, on the one hand, free elections, and to deny on the other hand 'one man one vote', is either a lie in the soul or an unpardonable illogicality in the head. 'One man one vote' is, and should be, the servant of 'the will of the people'. The denial of 'one man one vote' militates against the very idea of free elections, and makes a mockery of the same idea. One man one vote is fully consonant with the fundamental principle of people-centredness.

We have already referred to the fact that there is a constant and unfriendly conversation between people-centredness and ruler-centredness even in a democratic country. People freely choose their own rulers, but once in power the rulers start conditioning the electors to their own wishes or ways of doing things which are intended to keep them in power for as long as it is practicable. It is not unusual that towards election time the centre of gravity shifts heavily towards people-centredness, but after elections it shifts back to ruler-centredness, and as more power is given to the rulers it finally settles there until it no longer reflects 'the will of the people' but only their tolerance. And if this goes on unchecked by free discussions, free elections, and free criticism, people soon submit themselves to a ruler-centred system, and in this way establish a popularly elected dictatorship, or 'an elected tyranny'. It is self-evident that free discussions, free elections, and free criticism tend to keep the threat of ruler-centredness well under control and hence to protect, promote, and preserve people-centredness.

Two substantives have been used here—'will' and 'tolerance'. A brief examination of these symbols will not be out of place since these symbols are relevant to our discussion on the desirable system. In a people-centred system the rulers are elected by the people at free elections. Rulers depend on the free will of the people if they are to get and remain in power. What is this 'will'? It may mean two things. The power to choose or elect is 'will'. In this sense therefore 'the will of the people' means 'the power of the people to choose or elect'. 'Will' also means the choice which is made. 'The will of the people', therefore, means 'the choice of the people'. This twofold meaning of 'the will of the people' should be constantly kept in mind. If the people have freely elected those in power and those in power are the people's choice, then the principal of people-centredness is observed. This is politically sound as it makes for national stability.

But a stage may be reached when those who have been freely elected, who are the people's choice, may only be tolerated, although they may still think they are in power on the basis of 'the will of the people', when in fact 'the will of the people' has long degenerated into 'the tolerance of the people'. 'Tolerance' is not the same thing as 'will'. 'Tolerance' means the power or capacity of enduring; it may mean the endurance of offensive persons or opinions or government. A government that is based not on 'the will of the people' but on 'the tolerance of the people' cannot hope to bring about national stability. A tolerated government is allowed but not wholly approved. Once a stage is reached when 'the will of the people' has degenerated into 'the tolerance of the people' the next step is a desire to over-throw the government, and if there are no constitutional ways of doing this, there are always many unconstitutional ways of doing it. Many revolutions and military coups could have been prevented at the point of 'the tolerance of the people' if only free discussions, free elections, and free criticism had been allowed, and if those who held the reins of government had been sensitive enough to popular demands. A government is safe at the point of 'the will of the people', but once the mercury drops down to 'the tolerance of the people' a danger point is reached.

2. In order that the system serve the interests of the people it should

be fair but firm and flexible. A rigid system tends to break down. There has indeed to be a certain amount of conformity if things are to hang together in the interests of the nation, but it must be conformity within diversity rather than in uniformity. A rigid system ill suits a dynamic or changing situation. Even people within the same culture do not see things the same way, and they do not respond to these things in the same way. A too rigid system will only serve to provoke the people unnecessarily, whereas a flexible system, by its very nature, tends to allow all shades of political opinions and political behaviour to be expressed. Experience has shown that while national regimentation is impressive and delights the eye and appeals to our sense of precision, conformity, and uniformity, and gives us a sense of national unity, none the less flexible systems have the merit of outlasting rigid systems. By nature, flexible trees tend to survive storms, and trees that are too rigid to bend, break. Rigidity, in the present age of technological changes, cultural diffusion, general enlightenment, and differing and varying philosophies, appears to cut across the grain of the time. A flexible system seems to hold bright prospects in that it will at least allow free elections, free discussions, and free criticism and therefore adjust itself more effectively in accordance with popular demands and aspirations. But of course a flexible system is not the same thing as a weak system. It is a system that is elastic enough to absorb national shocks and thus prevent national disaster, resulting in the clash of the wills of the ruled and the rulers. The hallmark of a flexible system is tolerance.

3. The system should not be a personal one. It should be such that individual rulers may come and go, but it will continue long after individual rulers are dead and forgotten. A nation-centred system ensures national continuity and stability whereas personal rule does not seem to assure the same thing. Impersonal rule makes for higher efficiency which should be the goal of every nation.

It is clear from what has been said that what is important is not the one-party system or the two-party system or the multi-party system, but that whatever the system, people must have a say in the affairs of their country; they must have free elections; they must be allowed free discussions; they must be allowed free criticism; they must be allowed to express their own opinion freely. If this is done, then the fundamental principle of people-centredness will be fully implemented. Only such a system can consolidate effectively the many gains that African nationalism has made over the last two decades.

CHAPTER 20

West or East?

A great question is being posed by the great powers. Whither Africa? West or East? This question is often asked as if there was nowhere else Africa can go: either she goes West and not East, or she goes East and not West. This attitude is much to be regretted in that it seems to disregard altogether that free and independent Africa has a right to her own ways. It seems to assume that Africa has no right to existence unless she is appended to either the West or the East. The philosophy of 'the African personality', which has been so much projected by Dr. Kwame Nkrumah in his speeches and in his writings, is an attempt to correct this erroneous attitude.

When *African Nationalism* was first written in 1957, I said: 'The question is not whether Africans prefer European imperialism to Russian communism, or vice versa. They prefer neither.' This position is still true today (1967) as events in Africa seem to prove.

The whole purpose of African nationalism was not to destroy Western imperialism in order to make room for the Eastern bloc, or to deliver free and independent Africa back to the West. The purpose of African nationalism was to create a free and independent Africa with a distinct posture of its own, befriending both the West and the East but bowing down to neither. She must maintain her own integrity and a non-alignment policy is a device of ensuring this African integrity. The cold war between the West and the East is a power struggle between two giant powers and Africa will not allow herself to be a pawn in this power struggle. When two giant elephants start fighting, it would be futile for two hares to try to take sides in the fight. A policy of non-alignment would be practical wisdom. In any case, free and independent Africa should be busy with her own problems posed by the fact of independence. It is conceivable that a non-alignment bloc may hold the balance of power and hence save the two power blocs from dragging the world into another world war which could be far worse than World War II in which 28,000,000 people were killed.

Capitalism and communism are usually identified as irreconcilable enemies determined to liquidate each other. Sometimes they make an uneasy truce internationally known as co-existence, which presupposes that both capitalism and communism, the first representing the West, and the second the East, can live side by side with each other, but at the next available moment each starts undermining the other in spite of the co-existence truce! Each side starts wooing African countries to be on its side for no other reason than to get support in its fight against its eternal enemy. African countries, undeveloped and underdeveloped as they are, cannot afford this big power luxury of cold war. They must attend to the basic essentials that their countries so badly need.

Capitalists believe sincerely that their system can and does solve many economic problems that face any country. They have a proud record of real achievements which seem to have brought heaven on earth. The United States of America, which enjoys the highest standard of living in the world, has solved some of its numerous problems by the application of capitalism. Adam Smith, in his *Wealth of Nations* (1776), laid down the principle which capitalistic practices seem to have faithfully followed. He said:

Every individual endeavours to employ his capital so that its produce may be of greatest value. He generally, indeed, neither intends to promote the public interest, nor knows how much he is promoting it. ... He intends only his own security ... only his own gain, and he is in this, as in many other cases, led by an invisible hand to promote an end which was no part of his intention. ... By pursuing his own interest he frequently promotes that of the society more effectually than when he really intends to promote it.

The capitalistic system allows private enterprise and, judging by the amazing high standards of efficiency without governmental control, regulation, and direction, this seems to yield the satisfaction most people would look for in this world. My stay in the United States of America left me in no doubt that the capitalistic system there, whatever its deficiencies may be, works well, and the majority of people there are contented with that system.

On the other hand we have communists. They also sincerely believe that their economic system works wonders in their countries. I visited Communist China for four weeks to see things for myself. I visited Nanking, Peking, and Shanghai. I made a special point of visiting the communes and the factories there. I also visited many educational centres: primary and secondary schools as well as universities. I also visited the Peking Central Prison and hospitals, in one of which I was treated for tooth trouble and malaria fever. I had a series of discussions with very knowledgeable and experienced men the human warmth of whose hearts I have found elsewhere in the world—in the United States, Great Britain, Europe, and Africa. I was impressed by the way they had successfully tackled their many problems in the past and by the way they were tackling them in the present. They were applying communism to tackle problems that were facing 700,000,000! No objective observer can fail to appreciate that communism has worked wonders for the Chinese. The ordinary man is relatively much better off than before the communist régime took over in 1949. Communism is a system that has actually worked for the 700,000,000 Chinese, the 300,000,000 Russians, and millions of others. This, however, is not to say that communism has achieved the very high standard of living of some of the Western countries. Capitalism has been on the scene for a much longer time than communism. But both systems have been used successfully to solve problems that were facing millions of people. In the West capitalism has helped the have-nots to have something to live for. Similarly, in the East communism has also helped the have-nots to have something to live for. In other words, communism has been just as effective in the East as capitalism has been in the West, especially the United States. They have been effective systems if we take functionalism or pragmatism as our criterion.

But what has all this to do with the question Whither Africa? Capitalists sincerely believe that the economic problems facing free and independent Africa can be best solved by the application of capitalism: after all, capitalism has actually solved their own problems. Communists also sincerely believe that the many problems which face Africa can be better solved by the application of communism. Communists fear that if Africa adopts the capitalistic system, the majority of the peoples of Africa will continue to live in dire poverty. On the other hand, however, capitalists feel that communism in Africa will not really further the interests of the African people but those of communism. When two giant powers disagree who shall decide? Africa must decide since she is the one really affected in the whole matter. This is one approach to the tension between the West and the East in their quarrel over Africa—the supposed prize, according to the view of the big power blocs, that must be won by either the West or the East. Africa is not, and she cannot be, and she should not, and she must not be, any country's prize. The 260,000,000 peoples of Africa cannot be expected to play the role of furthering either capitalism or communism. They are there first and foremost to further their own interests. This is an important point that African political thinkers, ideologists, and political practitioners have to bear in mind, otherwise the peoples of Africa will not reap the benefits from the enormous gains that African nationalism has made. African nationalism won freedom and independence for the benefit of Africa, not for that of the West or East. Africa seeks the friendship of both the West and the East, but she seeks the domination of neither.

Africa cannot afford to approach her problems on the basis of an either/or proposition under pressure of West or East or from any other source. While in the past she had a system that satisfied the few needs of a primitive economy, the same cannot be said of Africa today. She has not as yet developed a clear, practical system of her own which can solve her many needs. A lot of good things can be learned from both capitalism and communism, and a lot could be used to solve certain problems, but it would appear that no 'package-deal' capitalism or communism can provide a wholesale solution to Africa's problems.

What would happen if free and independent Africa adopted a capitalistic system as represented by American capitalism? Capitalism by definition means that capital shall be in the hands of individuals. This is to say, all factors of production remain in private hands. Perhaps in highly developed countries, with long industrial experience there may not be dangers. But capitalism would mean that capital was in the hands of the individuals, and since individuals in Africa do not have real capital to speak of, it would have to be in the hands of foreign individuals, and this in turn would mean that most of the economy of the country would have to be controlled by foreign interests; the whole country therefore would have to dance to a foreign tune. This is the real danger of full-blown capitalism in Africa.

The whole idea behind capitalism is to make profit, and if the bulk of the capital is foreign, the bulk of the profits would accordingly leave the country. It would not be ploughed back into the country in the form of social services. Free enterprise in any African country is bound to expose the capital-lacking African people to the mercy of foreigners who have much capital, so that the present system that exploits the African people would continue long after freedom and independence had been won.

Suppose full-blown communism was introduced in Africa on a Chinese style, what would happen? Basing the observation on the situation of communism in China, it might be said that the enormity of the problem facing 700,000,000 people could not be solved in any other way than by a regimental system like that characterizing communism in the People's Republic of China. They had to adopt communism to survive—and people co-operated because it promised them a solution to their problems. They gave up a great deal of their private property because the situation demanded it. The needs of the stupefying numbers could be better met by a system of regimentation which was not geared to the private profit motive. 700,000,000 mouths had to be fed sufficiently, and it did not matter that that feeding came via regimentation.

Africa has no such numbers to deal with at present. She is sparsely populated. She has only 260,000,000 people in 11,500,000 square miles whereas the People's Republic of China has 700,000,000 people on 3,876,956 square miles of land. People in a heavily populated country like the People's Republic of China may find it necessary to respond to regimentation in their own interests, whereas people in a sparsely populated continent like Africa may find it quite unnecessary to co-operate in regimental measures. Communism therefore cannot be taken so readily in Africa because of different temperaments and attitudes resulting from actual life situations. This, however, is not to say that Africa has nothing to borrow and to take from communism. It has a lot to learn from both communism and capitalism, but this cannot be on the basis of a 'package deal'.

Even if Africa desired to imbibe capitalism or communism hook, line, and sinker, she could not do so since each system is grounded in, and supported by, attitudes based in history. Capitalism is the sum total of Western economic experience, and communism is also the sum total of economic experience. Africa cannot live the experiences of others. She has to live her own experiences and out of these will emerge a system suited to African needs, to African temperament, and to African imagination and capacity. Even if Africa really desired to follow American capitalism it would be impossible since only an American situation can produce American capitalism. Even if she desired to follow Russian or Chinese communism she would still fail to achieve her goal since it requires a Russian or Chinese situation to produce Russian or Chinese communism. Any people are entitled to their own attitudes towards this or that institution, but for either the West or the East to invite Africa to repeat their attitudes is to assume that Africa has no attitudes of her own. If she adopts either capitalism or communism or a mixture of both, such a system must reflect African attitudes and values.

Africa has her own destiny. Other continents should not treat her as though she was the rubber-stamp of either capitalism or communism. Africa's non-alignment policy can have no other meaning than that Africa simply refuses to play the role of a rubber-stamp. Both capitalism and communism are in many ways corrective of each other, and it would appear that the deep tension between capitalism and communism leaves enough room for a third alternative. Between capitalism's fundamental principle of 'exploitation of man by man' and communism's 'inevitable conflict between man and man' there should and there must be a third alternative, and with patience, calculated economic planning, and foresight Africa can evolve a system which, while meeting her own basic needs, would also diminish the tension between capitalism and communism.

Too often when independent African countries get help from the Eastern bloc, the Western bloc is seized with hysteria, although between the West and the East there is considerable foreign trade. They seem to assume that it is their right to deal with communist countries, but not the right of the African countries to do so. Similarly the eastern bloc, when it sees African countries dealing with the Western bloc, cries 'Imperialist stooges!' If only both sides could remember that Africa is not on sale! If only they could remember that there is a third alternative for Africa! If a large placard, bearing the words, 'HANDS OFF AFRICA!' could be placed at every African port and airport, perhaps this would remind both West and East that Africa intends solving her problems in her own way in the light of her history, her experiences and outlook on life. Yes, to be helped by either the West or the East, or by both, Africa likes, but neither the domination of the West nor that of the East does she like.

In the struggle for the liberation of Africa, African nationalism has not hesitated to accept help from any quarter. Communist help has been accepted from time to time to effect the liberation of the African continent from the shackles and fetters of colonialism. Help has also been accepted from capitalist countries for the same reason. Even if help had come from the Devil himself, African nationalism would not have hesitated in accepting it. Imagine a man sinking in a river. He cries for help. Someone stretches out a helping hand. The sinking man would not be interested in knowing whether or not the helping hand was from the West or from the East. What is material to the sinking man is that it is a 'helping hand'. A capitalist may be worried that the help came from communist countries. Similarly, a communist may be perturbed that help came from capitalist countries. But it is not Africa's worry. The emphasis of African nationalism is on 'help' while that of the two blocs is on 'source' of the help.

It is clear that African nationalists do not accept Western and Eastern help so that they become capitalists or communists. They do so to help themselves first and foremost. They have no intention of furthering either capitalism or communism. When the American colonists asked for French help during the American Revolutionary Wars, they were not by that act asking to become French. They were merely asking for French help to dislodge British control over their own affairs, and to reassert the integrity they had assumed. When the Soviet Union and the Allied Powers joined hands against Nazi Germany this was not an invitation to any of the parties to lose their national identity and assume that of another. It was a method of meeting effectively a highly threatening situation. Similarly, African nationalists have their own ways of asking for help to meet situations that threaten them with non-freedom, non-citizenship, and humiliation in their own countries. Effective help wherever it comes from has proved to be a practical way of handling practical problems.

If, after the help has been given, an African country so helped decides to become capitalist or communist, this would be a co-incidence. But should a country so decide this would be its own way of solving the problems that face it, and every country is entitled to its own formula of solving the many problems that face it as long as such methods that are used do not outrage humanity.

African nationalism has been fundamentally interested in liberating the continent of Africa, and it has not failed to utilize to full extent the tension between capitalism and communism, who have been the joint midwives of African independence. Whither Africa? To the West or to the East? Our answer is an emphatic one and it is, 'Neither.'

CHAPTER 21

African Socialism

In this chapter an economic system which would solve the many problems that face Africa will be discussed. First, the fundamental principle of people-centredness in contradistinction to ruler-centredness and to profit-centredness must be reasserted. It is necessary to follow African thinking in relation to a workable economic system to be hammered out on the anvil of African circumstances.

What is socialism? Socialism as a theory has something to do with the relationships between facts or with the ordering of these facts into a meaningful arrangement or whole. These facts are, first, the people themselves; secondly, the means of production; and thirdly, the means of distribution. In other words, socialism as a theory seeks to order the relationships between the people and the means of production and the means of distribution so that maximum economic benefit accrues to the maximum number.

President Julius Nyerere of Tanzania said his fellow countrymen could understand socialism only as co-operation. He did not say 'on the basis of compulsion or force or regimentation'. In some countries socialism uses ruthless force to make headway. A socialism that is based on the willing co-operation of the people accords to our fundamental principle of people-centredness.

President Senghor of Senegal, speaking at the Dakar Conference in December 1962 on the 'African Roads to Socialism', said: 'Socialism is the merciless fight against social dishonesties and injustices; fraudulent conversion of public funds, rackets, and bribes.' In spite of this negative definition of socialism one thing remains clear, and that is that socialism is intended for the benefit of the people as a whole.

But Dr. Nyerere struck a deeper and profounder note when he said:

The foundation, and the objective, of African socialism is the extended family. The true African socialist does not look on one class of men as his brethren and another as his natural enemies. He does not form an alliance with the 'brethren' for the extermination of the 'non-brethren'. He rather regards all men as his brethren—as members of his ever extending family. . . .

Ujamaa, then, or 'familyhood', describes our socialism. It is opposed to capitalism, which seeks to build a happy society on the basis of the exploitation of man by man; and it is equally opposed to doctrinaire socialism which seeks to build its happy society on a philosophy of inevitable conflict between man and man.[1]

A few points on these two statements should be clarified. According to Dr. Nyerere the extended family is both the foundation and the objective of African Socialism. If historical experience is something to go by, all peoples of the earth have at one stage or another during their development enjoyed the existence of the extended family, which has been destroyed by the process and the volume of industrialization and urbanization. Today the conjugal family seems to be pushing the consanguineal family into the background, and this naturally militates against African Socialism which is based on the extended family. How to industrialize without destroying the idea of the extended family is a real problem facing African Socialists.

Dr. Nyerere repudiated the vicious practice of the 'brethren' forming an alliance to exterminate the 'non-brethren'. The idea of a human family—of regarding all men as members of an ever extending family—accords with the fundamental principle of people-centredness. It is the people who are important and not the system; it is the system that should serve, and not oppress, man.

But Dr. Nyerere went to the heart of the matter when, in the second paragraph quoted, he repudiated the idea of 'a happy society' built on the principle of 'the exploitation of man by man', and the idea of 'a happy society' built on the concept of 'inevitable conflict between man and man'. He could not have been more people-centred than this, and it is this people-centredness that is the very heart of African Socialism. People are more important than ideologies or systems or things. Profits cannot be more important than people. People cannot be exterminated in order to enforce an ideology or a doctrine. People cannot be treated like things in order to make super-profits. Neither profit nor doctrine can be allowed to be the centre of things. People are to be the centre of things. This is African Socialism.

Tom Mboya had this to say about African Socialism:

In Africa the belief that 'we are all sons and daughters of the soil' has always exercised tremendous influence on our social, economic and political relationships. From this belief spring the logic and the prac-

[1] Julius Nyerere, *Freedom and Unity: Uhuru na Umoja*, Oxford University Press, London, 1967, p. 170.

tice of equality, and the acceptance of communal ownership of the vital means of life—the land. The hoe is to us the symbol of work. Every able-bodied man and woman, girl and boy, has always worked. ... There has been equality of opportunity, for everyone had land—or rather the use of land—and a hoe at the start of life. The acquisitive instinct, which is largely responsible for the vicious excesses and exploitation under the capitalist system, was tempered by a sense of togetherness and a rejection of craft and meanness. There was loyalty to the society, and the society gave its members much in return: a sense of security and universal hospitality.[1]

Tom Mboya posed a fundamental concept—'sons and daughters of the soil'—as a basis of African Socialism. This concept presupposes brotherhood and sisterhood of all those who draw their subsistence from a common soil. This common brotherhood and common sisterhood of men and women, in the same country, in turn, implies a common 'familyhood', to use Dr. Nyerere's concept. From the concept of 'sons and daughters of the soil' flows equality of persons. The principle of communal ownership of land takes its full meaning from the concept of 'sons and daughters of the soil'. These may be repeated for the sake of a clear exposition—a common brotherhood and sisterhood, a common equality of persons, a common ownership of land, a common equality of opportunity, a common practice of work, a common sense of togetherness, a common rejection of craft and meanness, a common sense of loyalty to society, a common sense of security, and a common hospitality. In other words, familyhood, equality of persons, communal ownership of land, equality of opportunity, honest work, a sense of togetherness, a rejection of craft and meanness, a loyalty of society, a sense of security, and universal hospitality are the bases of African Socialism.

If these ten concepts are examined it will be found that every one of them gravitates around the fundamental principle of people-centredness. It is important to note that Tom Mboya's bases of African Socialism are strongly geared to good human relationships. Equality in all its dimensions can only be conceivable in the realm of human relationships. So are communal ownership, togetherness, loyalty, security, hospitality, and brotherhood and sisterhood. President Sékou Touré of Guinea said:

The socialist régime should develop that high standard of [social] consciousness through its essentially democratic, popular and pro-

[1] Tom Mboya, *Freedom and After*, André Deutsch, London, 1963, p. 163.

gressive organization and the socialist quality of its human relations.
. . . This is the place to affirm unequivocally our belief in the inevitable socialization of world society. Our experiment is an endeavour
of a new type to achieve a socialist development starting from an
agrarian background. . . . Our course is a non-capitalistic course, and
so it will remain. . . . To achieve harmony between the living conditions of all the peoples on earth, a number of essentials have to be
fulfilled. This harmonization, if it is to be valuable and beneficial to
world society, should be effected with a view to general progress, and
not to levelling out the most advanced and the least developed societies.[1]

Political doctrines, social philosophies and economic systems should
not be regarded as anything else but 'means' placed at the disposal
of man and society for serving their permanent interest in fulfilling
their rightful aspirations to full expression of the personality and the
unfolding of man's political, economic, intellectual, physical and
moral capacities. . . . Thus, in choosing our objectives, forms of
organization and methods of working, we choose first and foremost
'ourselves', our future, our happiness, for the sake of which all else is
'means'. . . . The path we have chosen for our development rules out
from our society—let us repeat—any relationship of inequality and
subordination, and any practice of exploitation of man by man. . . .
There is much talk of 'African socialism', and this seems to infer that
there also exists a Chinese socialism, an American socialism, a Yugo-
slavian or Bulgarian socialism. . . . Why would people, tomorrow, not
talk of the Nigerian or Togolese path of African socialism . . . ? Is
socialism a means, or is it an end in itself? The P.D.G., on its part,
thinks that socialism is a means, and that the end which deserves our
attention, justifies our mobilization, and inspires our struggle, is the
moral and material happiness of the people. It is with this end in view
that we choose our social structures, our economic and cultural
patterns. . . . Engaging in 'socialism for the sake of socialism' is trying
to mow with the sickle's handle.[2]

Sékou Touré's views are very relevant to African Socialist thinking.
He believes in the inevitability of universal socialization. The fundamental principle of socialism is the vesting of the means of production
and distribution in the hands of the community or the State.
Sékou Touré does not accept the capitalist thesis of the exploitation
of man by man. Nor does he believe in social inequality and subordination of man to man or of one class to another.

Sékou Touré believes in the harmonization of living conditions.

[1] Sékou Touré, *Guinean Revolution and Social Progress*, S.O.P. Press,
Cairo, pp. 18 and 361–2.
[2] Sékou Touré, op. cit., p. 322.

This is another aspect of 'socialization'. To 'harmonize' means to bring peace and friendship; to remove contradictions or inconsistencies or inequalities or injustices; to adjust in fit proportions; to agree in action or adaptation. To harmonize living conditions would therefore appear to mean the removal of all social injustices and the establishment of social justice. Perhaps we could venture beyond this point and spell out 'living conditions' as having reference to food, shelter, clothing, transport, schooling, hospitalization, and the like. The task of harmonizing living conditions is therefore to correct the discrepancy between the 'haves' and the 'have-nots', not to convert the 'haves' into the 'have-nots'.

Sékou Touré holds that socialism is a means to man's ends. Man is not a means to socialism's ends. Because he believes that socialism is a means he holds that socialism is adaptable to African conditions. There is therefore no blue-print socialism since it is a means to 'ourselves, our future and our happiness'.

When we take the various elements of Sékou Touré's socialist thinking—universal socialization, no capitalistic system, rejection of exploitation of man by man, repudiation of a condition or state of inequality and subordination, harmonization of living conditions, his belief that socialism is a means to an end and not an end in itself and his rejection of the subordination of man to ideologies, we see clearly that this accords with the fundamental principle of people-centredness.

Dr. Kwame Nkrumah said:

I maintain that there is no universal pattern for industrialization that can serve as an absolute model for new nations emerging out of colonialism. Looking around, we find no examples that are identical. European countries stretched their industrialization over a much longer period and in a different economic, scientific and social epoch. The United States cleared virgin land and used slave labour to amass its primary wealth. It has a geographical span that gave it special opportunities for a rapid industrial expansion and large scale of manufacture. The Soviet Union, starting from practically nothing, covering a vast land mass with manifold resources, swept away the former bureaucracy, and employed an authoritarian dictatorship to achieve its purpose.

In Ghana, we have embarked on the socialist path to progress. We want to see full employment, good housing, and equal opportunity for education and cultural advancement for all the people up to the highest level possible. This means that:
— prices of goods must not exceed wages;
— house rentals must be within the means of all groups;

— social welfare services must be open to all;

— educational and cultural amenities must be available to everyone. It means, in short, that the real income and standard of life of all farmers and workers must rise appreciably. . . . Production for private profit deprives a large section of the people of the goods and services produced. If, therefore, we are to fulfil our pledge to the people and achieve the programme set out above, socialism is our only alternative. For socialism assumes the public ownership of the means of production, the land and its resources and the use of those means in fulfilment of the people's needs.

Socialism . . . is predicted upon the ability to satisfy those needs. . . .

. . . Our aim is the building of a society in which the principles of social justice will be paramount. But there are many roads to socialism. . . .[1]

Like Sékou Touré, Dr. Nkrumah does not subscribe to the view that there is a universal pattern of socialism. For Dr. Nkrumah socialism is a practical formula of progress which cannot be understood apart from the exercise of satisfying the needs of the people. It is, to cast Dr. Nkrumah's thinking into Sékou Touré's mould, a 'means' of satisfying the people's needs. Since this is socialism's main objective it cuts across the profit motive which dominates the capitalistic system. Social justice is to be paramount in Dr. Nkrumah's socialism. His concept of 'social justice' would appear to accord with Sékou Touré's concept of 'harmonizing living conditions'. Socialism seeks to create equality of opportunity in the various departments of life. Dr. Nkrumah clearly advocates public ownership of the means of production, and this stems from his acceptance of socialism as something that can improve the lot of the people, and cure the many ills caused by the exploitative capitalistic system.

It may be well to recapitulate what each of these four African leaders holds in the main:

1. Dr. Nyerere's socialism is based principally on the fundamental concept of the universal brotherhood of man as evidenced by a common familyhood; on the repudiation of capitalism's society built on the exploitation of man by man; and on the rejection of doctrinaire socialism's society built on inevitable conflict between man and man.

2. Tom Mboya's socialism is built around a common fellowship expressed in the idea of 'sons and daughters of the soil'. It is built

[1] Kwame Nkrumah, *Africa Must Unite*, Heinemann Educational Books Ltd., London, pp. 118–21.

around a communal ownership of land, a common equality, and a common loyalty to society.

3. Sékou Touré's socialism is built around the concepts of universal socialization, harmonization of living conditions, and the rejection of the capitalistic system, inequality between man and man, and insubordination of man to man. It rejects the subordination of man to ideologies, regarding these as subordinate to man.

4. Dr. Nkrumah's socialism is a means to an end and not an end in itself. Its whole purpose is to satisfy the people's needs by eliminating capitalism's profit motive and placing the means of production under public ownership and control.

All these four samples of socialist thinking have certain things in common. First, there is a strong emphasis on people as people (people-centredness). Secondly, there is a strong feeling against the capitalistic system. Thirdly, there is an equally strong feeling against doctrinaire socialism exalted above man. There is a clear and decided rejection of absolute socialism, but there is a ready acceptance of a relative, adaptable socialism. Fourthly, there is a readiness to maximize social benefits for the maximum number.

Why are the African leaders so much against the capitalistic system? Free and independent Africa has been thoroughly conditioned against capitalism. European capital in Africa has been used to exploit not only the natural resources but also the human resources in order to produce super-profits. In the process of achieving super-profits capitalism usually treated Africans as things and not as persons—as a means to achieve super-profits. As long as capitalism remained firmly in the saddle the majority suffered and lost their human status for a time. Black capitalists are just as bad as white capitalists. Capitalism has nothing to do with this or that race. All capitalists—black, white, yellow, or brown—come from the same cannibal mother. Socialism is an effort to remedy this cannibalism inherent in capitalism. It is clear why African leaders, who have been victims of capitalism, and whose countries have been a free field of capitalistic exploitation are so much set against capitalism as practised in the West.

But there is another reason for this African anti-capitalistic attitude. The various African countries have not at their disposal the necessary capital among their own citizens. They cannot engage in capitalistic activities without sacrificing the welfare of their own people to the super-profit seekers. They are compelled by circumstances to have a planned economy or to perpetuate capitalism with all its exploitative evils.

How is it that while African leaders are ready to embrace socialism, they have done so with a great deal of care ? African socialist thinkers are opposed to 'doctrinaire' socialism. Just as they are saying, 'Capitalism—hands off Africa!', so are they also saying, 'Doctrinaire socialism—hands of Africa!' They do not accept the thesis that there is, or there should be, a blue-print socialism. To them socialism is relative not absolute.

It would appear that among the African people there is no real resistance to the introduction of socialism since there are no million-aires and other big financial magnates. The tendency is therefore to take people steadily along the path of socialism without the rigours and deprivations of 'doctrinaire' socialism. Africa has nothing to lose by the introduction of socialism. The people are ripe for such a system. All countries in Africa, except for Rwanda and Burundi, are under-populated, and the introduction of socialism becomes a rela-tively easy matter.

It is not part of the make-up of the peoples of Africa to resort to rigorous measures of conformity which are demanded by 'doctrin-aire' socialism. Their spiritual world still has a powerful hold on their minds. A man cannot be lightly killed. To plan the extermination of people because they did not adhere to a certain doctrine is not a general characteristic of the African people. In Africa people want to live as they like, not as their rulers like, and the rulers can only bring about the necessary socialist measures through the practical needs of the people. 'Doctrinaire' socialism would inevitably cause a showdown between the people and their rulers, and Africa cannot afford running this risk. She has enough problems already on her hands. There is therefore much practical wisdom in Africa's re-pudiation of 'doctrinaire' socialism.

Let it be remembered that African Socialism looks forward to the day when African society will cease to exist as a vast field of exploita-tion by individual and foreign interests. The newly independent African countries cannot afford the luxury of *laissez-faire* economies without delivering the people back into the crushing jaws of colonial capitalism and black capitalism. The interests of Africa will be best served not by a profit-centred economic system, but by a people-centred system, and African Socialism is that system.

PD-6682-L
5-25
CO

PB-6882-4
5-25
CC